PIRATE

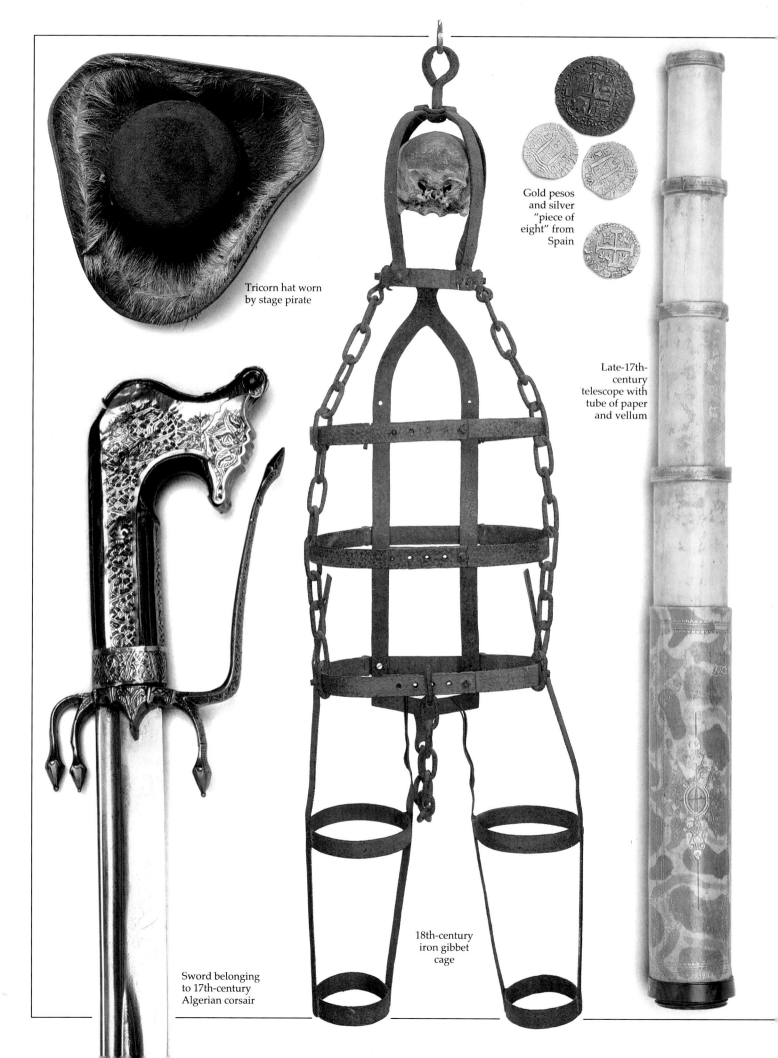

Tricorn hat worn
by stage pirate

Gold pesos
and silver
"piece of
eight" from
Spain

Late-17th-
century
telescope with
tube of paper
and vellum

18th-century
iron gibbet
cage

Sword belonging
to 17th-century
Algerian corsair

Ring with skull-
and-crossbones
motif

DK EYEWITNESS GUIDES

PIRATE

Gold
rings taken as
pirates' booty

Written by
RICHARD PLATT

Photographed by
TINA CHAMBERS

Sloop, the
type of vessel
used by pirates
in the Caribbean

Powder flask
with the cross
of the Knights
of St John

DK

DORLING KINDERSLEY
London • New York • Stuttgart

In association with
THE NATIONAL MARITIME MUSEUM, LONDON

Mariner's compass
with ivory case

Pair of flintlock pistols

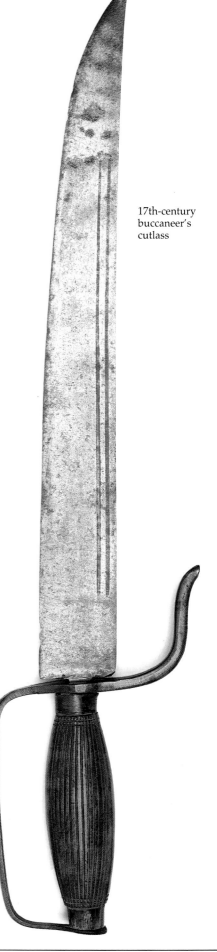

17th-century
buccaneer's
cutlass

DK

A DORLING KINDERSLEY BOOK

Project editor Bridget Hopkinson
Art editor Ann Cannings
Managing editor Simon Adams
Managing art editor Julia Harris
Researcher Céline Carez
Production Catherine Semark
Picture research Giselle Harvey
Consultant David Cordingly

This Eyewitness ® Guide has been conceived by
Dorling Kindersley Limited and Editions Gallimard

First published in Great Britain in 1995
by Dorling Kindersley Limited,
9 Henrietta Street, London WC2E 8PS

6 8 10 9 7

A CIP catalogue record for this book is
available from the British Library.

ISBN 0 7513 6035 X

Filmsetting by Litho Link Ltd,
Welshpool, Powys

Colour reproduction by Colourscan, Singapore
Printed in China
by Toppan Printing Co., (Shenzhen) Ltd.

Cloak of a
17th-century
gentleman pirate

A navigator's
astronomical
compendium

A hoard of
pirate treasure

Contents

17th-century French treasure chest

Robbers of the seas

Who were the pirates? Daring figures who swooped on treasure ships and returned home with golden cargoes? Brutal sea-thieves who showed no mercy to their victims? Bold adventurers who financed travel by nautical theft? In fact they were all these things and more. The term "pirate" means simply "one who plunders on the sea", but those who led this life fell into several categories: "privateers" were sea-raiders with a government licence to pillage enemy ships; "buccaneers" were 17th-century pirates who menaced the Spanish in the Caribbean; "corsairs" were privateers and pirates who roved the Mediterranean. In the words of Bartholomew Roberts (p. 39), all were lured by the promise of "plenty..., pleasure..., liberty and power".

SWASHBUCKLING HERO
A few real pirates lived up to their traditional swashbuckling image. Bold and brilliant Welsh pirate Howell Davis used daring ruses to capture ships off Africa's Guinea coast in 1719.

A TEMPTING TARGET
The East Indiamen – big ships trading between Europe and Asia – provided some of the toughest but most tempting targets for pirates. In earlier times, the capture of a Spanish galleon bringing treasure from the Americas was many a pirate's sweetest dream.

Wealthy East India Companies decorated the sterns of their merchantmen with gold

PIRATES OF THE SILVER SCREEN
Hollywood pirate films often blurred the lines between fact and fiction. In *Blackbeard the Pirate*, Blackbeard is pursued by Henry Morgan, who looks surprisingly well for a man who had in fact been dead for 30 years!

PROMISE OF RICHES
This illustration from Robert Louis Stevenson's famous pirate story *Treasure Island* (p.60) shows the heroes loading sacks full of pirate treasure. Although there were many myths surrounding piracy, the vast fortunes in gold and silver captured by some pirates really existed. Pirates could become millionaires overnight, but they usually spent their booty as soon as they acquired it.

Cannon is balanced on this circular pivot

Pushing wedge in aims cannon lower

A HARD LIFE
For sailors of the 17th- and 18th-centuries, life at sea was hard and dangerous and, like "Poor Jack" in this poem, many never made it home again. Seamen were often tricked or kidnapped by press gangs into serving on men-of-war where they were subjected to appalling conditions and harsh discipline. Compared to this, a pirate's life offered freedom and easy money and many pirate crews were made up of formerly honest seamen.

"Poor Jack" going away to sea, perhaps never to return

POOR JACK.

PIRATES OF THE IMAGINATION
Pirates have captured the imaginations of many writers and artists over the years. The American illustrator Howard Pyle portrayed the pirates and buccaneers of the 17th century in colourful and authentic detail. This evocative picture epitomizes the traditional image of the flamboyant pirate captain.

A rope was attached to the end of the grappling iron

RULE OF TERROR
Pirates had a reputation for cruelty, which many of them encouraged. They knew that their victims would surrender more easily if resistance was punished by torture and death. The buccaneers in particular were notorious for their brutality.

BARBAROUS BRUTES?
The definition of a "pirate" often depended on which country you belonged to. This painting shows evil-looking Barbary corsairs attacking a helpless English crew. To the Europeans the Barbary corsairs were brutal heathen pirates, but in North Africa, they were seen as legal privateers.

DARING THE DEVIL
Popular pirate tales such as those found in Charles Elms' *The Pirate's Own Book* (p. 61) encouraged the "superstitious horror connected with the name of pirate". In this illustration from Elms' book a reckless pirate captain offers the devil a handful of his hair in return for a fair wind.

18th-century cannon that belonged to French corsair René Duguay-Trouin

DANGER SIGNAL
A cannon shot was the signal for a ship to show its colours or be treated as an enemy. Pirates often tricked their victims by running up the colours of a friendly nation.

GRAPPLING FOR GOLD
Swung into the rigging on the end of a rope, a grappling iron helped pirates to draw their victims' ship close enough for boarding. But pirates only did this as a last resort, preferring to make victims surrender by a show of force.

Barbed points are designed to lodge securely in the rigging of another ship

Pirates of Ancient Greece

SOME OF THE WORLD'S GREAT CIVILIZATIONS grew up around the Mediterranean and Aegean seas. Unfortunately for the peoples of the ancient world, these same waters were home to marauding "sea-robbers". The Aegean, at the centre of the Greek world, was ideal for pirates. They hid among its countless tiny islands and inlets, from where they could prey safely on passing trade ships. Piracy was fairly easy for these early sea raiders because merchant vessels hugged the coast and never crossed the open ocean. If the pirates waited long enough on a busy trade route, a valuable prize would soon sail around the headland. Pirates also attacked villages, kidnapping people to ransom or sell as slaves. As Greek city-states grew in power, they built navies which tried to keep the pirates under control.

PIRATE ATTACK
The painting on this Greek bowl shows early pirates in action. When it was painted 2,500 years ago, pirate attacks were common throughout the Aegean, and there was little distinction between piracy and warfare. Later, when Greek city-states tried to impose order, pirates disguised their raids as reprisals – the custom of retaliating against attacks without actually declaring war.

Lumbering merchant ship under full sail

Fast pirate galley powered by oars

Sharp ram of the pirate galley drives into the side of the merchant ship

Athenian drinking bowl, 6th century B.C.

ASSYRIAN GALLEY
The Assyrians, who lived in what is now Iraq, probably attacked pirates in the Mediterranean in ships like this. However, no one knows for sure exactly what these vessels looked like.

THE PHOENICIANS FIGHT BACK
The Phoenicians carried out a thriving maritime trade from the cities of Tyre and Sidon (in present day Lebanon) in the 7th and 6th centuries B.C. Their merchant ships carried luxury cargoes such as silver, tin, copper, and amber to every corner of the Mediterranean. However, Greek pirates were a serious threat to Phoenician shipping, and war galleys, such as the one shown on this Phoenician coin, right, were used to defend their trade interests.

Silver shekels from the
Phoenician city of Tyre

**A HOARD
OF SILVER**
Phoenician
ships
carrying luxury
goods around the
Mediterranean were
obvious targets for
early pirates. If they
were lucky, pirates might
capture a cargo of silver
from Spain, which was
used to make Phoenician
coins like these.

A PIRATE VESSEL OF ANCIENT GREECE
This atmospheric photograph shows a replica of a Greek pirate galley.
Pirates of the ancient world did not build special vessels, but relied on
what was locally available. They used all kinds of ships, but favoured
light, shallow-bottomed galleys that were fast and easy to manoeuvre.
If the pirates were pursued, their shallow boats enabled them to sail
over rocks close to the shore where larger vessels could not follow.

*Sennacherib's face has
been defaced by an
ancient vandal*

PIRATES IN MYTHOLOGY
A Greek myth tells of a band of
foolish pirates who captured
Dionysus, the god of wine,
hoping to ransom him. But the
god took on the shape of a lion,
and the terrified pirates threw
themselves into the sea. As a
punishment, Dionysus turned
the pirates into a school of
frolicking dolphins, pictured in
this mosaic. The same story
appears in Roman mythology,
but the god is called Bacchus.

SENNACHERIB, SCOURGE OF PIRATES
In 694 B.C. the Assyrian king Sennacherib (ruled 705–682 B.C.),
above, waged war against Chaldean sea raiders who had
taken refuge in his kingdom on the coast of Elam, at the
northern end of the Persian Gulf. His campaign successfully
ended this seaborne threat.

ALEXANDER THE GREAT
Pirates roamed the Aegean when
Alexander the Great (356–323 B.C.),
right, ruled over Greece. In
331 B.C. he ordered them to be
cleared from the seas. The great
warrior king reputedly asked a
captured pirate what reason he
had for making the seas unsafe.
The pirate replied: "The same
reason as you have for troubling
the whole world. But since I do it
in a small ship, I am called a pirate.
Because you do it with a great fleet,
you are called an emperor."

MEDITERRANEAN MERCHANT SHIP
Ancient Greek trading vessels were no match for the sleek,
streamlined galleys of the pirates who harassed them. Powered by
a square sail, they were easily overtaken
by the fast oar-driven pirate craft.

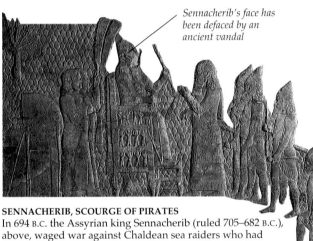

Terracotta model of a
merchant ship, 6th century B.C.

*Hull is broad and
rounded to provide
maximum cargo space*

Pirates of the Roman world

"SAIL IN AND UNLOAD, your cargo is already sold!" With this slogan the Aegean port of Delos lured merchant ships – and pirates. The bustling port was part of the great Roman empire, which flourished between about 200 B.C. and A.D. 476. In Delos market pirates sold kidnapped slaves and stolen cargoes to wealthy Romans who asked no questions. However, in the 1st century B.C. pirates posed a growing menace to trading vessels in the Mediterranean. When piracy threatened imports of grain to Rome, the people demanded action. In 67 B.C. a huge fleet of ships led by Pompey the Great rounded up the sea pirates, while the Roman army swooped on their base in Cilicia. This campaign solved Rome's immediate problems, but pirates remained a menace.

Deck rail

Oarsmen in the Roman navy were free men, not slaves

Lower deck was hot and smelly

Cutaway trireme

THE TRIREME
The warships that Rome sent against the pirates closely resembled Greek galleys. They were probably sleek triremes powered by three banks of oarsmen. Armed with a sharp ramming prow, these light vessels were fast and easy to handle in the calm waters of the Mediterranean. Their name means literally "three-er", probably because of the three-tier system of rowers.

KIDNAPPED
In about 75 B.C. the young Julius Caesar (c.102–44 B.C.) was captured by pirates while travelling to Rhodes to study. The pirates held him captive on a tiny Ionic island for more than five weeks until his ransom was paid. After his release, Caesar took his revenge by tracking down the pirates and crucifying them.

Silver denarius bearing Caesar's portrait

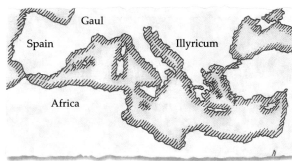

Gaul
Spain
Illyricum
Africa

ROMAN WORLD
This map shows how the Roman empire at its height stretched around the entire Mediterranean.

Corbita's hold might contain luxuries on its return from Italy

SLOW BOAT
Broad, rounded corbitae like this one made up the majority of Rome's grain fleet. Mediterranean pirates would have had little trouble hijacking these slow, heavily laden vessels as they sailed around the coast from Alexandria and Carthage to Ostia, the port that served Rome.

PRIZE WHEAT
Pirates attacking a Roman grain ship might be rewarded with a cache of emmer, above, a variety of wheat grown in the ancient world. Such cargoes could be sold at a profit in local markets.

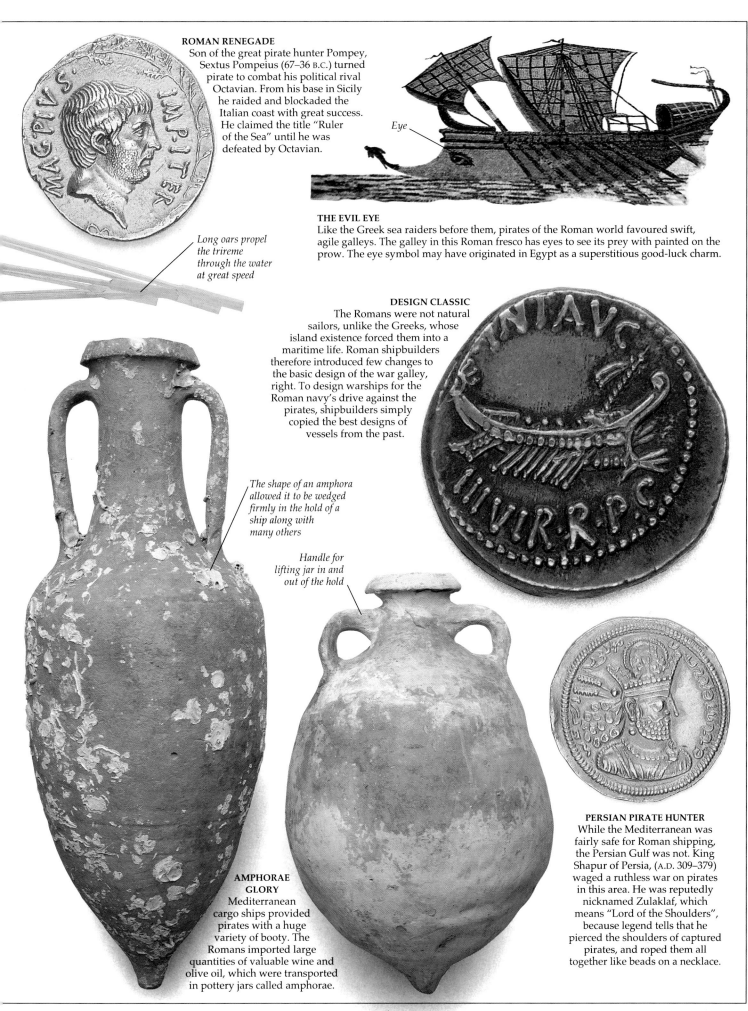

ROMAN RENEGADE
Son of the great pirate hunter Pompey, Sextus Pompeius (67–36 B.C.) turned pirate to combat his political rival Octavian. From his base in Sicily he raided and blockaded the Italian coast with great success. He claimed the title "Ruler of the Sea" until he was defeated by Octavian.

Eye

Long oars propel the trireme through the water at great speed

THE EVIL EYE
Like the Greek sea raiders before them, pirates of the Roman world favoured swift, agile galleys. The galley in this Roman fresco has eyes to see its prey with painted on the prow. The eye symbol may have originated in Egypt as a superstitious good-luck charm.

DESIGN CLASSIC
The Romans were not natural sailors, unlike the Greeks, whose island existence forced them into a maritime life. Roman shipbuilders therefore introduced few changes to the basic design of the war galley, right. To design warships for the Roman navy's drive against the pirates, shipbuilders simply copied the best designs of vessels from the past.

The shape of an amphora allowed it to be wedged firmly in the hold of a ship along with many others

Handle for lifting jar in and out of the hold

AMPHORAE GLORY
Mediterranean cargo ships provided pirates with a huge variety of booty. The Romans imported large quantities of valuable wine and olive oil, which were transported in pottery jars called amphorae.

PERSIAN PIRATE HUNTER
While the Mediterranean was fairly safe for Roman shipping, the Persian Gulf was not. King Shapur of Persia, (A.D. 309–379) waged a ruthless war on pirates in this area. He was reputedly nicknamed Zulaklaf, which means "Lord of the Shoulders", because legend tells that he pierced the shoulders of captured pirates, and roped them all together like beads on a necklace.

Raiders of the North

BOBBING ABOVE THE WAVES, the sail of a Viking ship struck terror into the people of 9th-century northern Europe. It warned that dangerous Viking pirates would soon land nearby. These fearsome Scandinavian warriors preyed on shipping and raided villages far inland. Since ancient times, the coastal tribes of Scandinavia had lived by robbing passing merchant ships. When they began to cross the open sea, it was natural for them to pillage the nearest foreign coasts. Viking ships roamed the North Sea in search of plunder, spreading fear and mayhem wherever they landed. The Vikings were not the first raiders of the North, nor the last. As long as merchant ships carried valuable cargoes, pirates were never far behind.

Viking arrow-heads

BATTLE AXE
The axe was the favourite weapon of the Vikings. In the hands of a seasoned warrior, the great two-handed broad-axe could fell a man with a single blow. For fighting at sea, Vikings preferred a medium-sized axe which was easy to handle when boarding another vessel.

Silver decoration indicates that this axe was a symbol of prestige and power

THE SAXON THREAT
Five centuries before the Vikings began to terrorize northern Europe, Saxon pirates from the Baltic Sea plagued coasts and shipping. The Saxon raiders forced England's Roman rulers to strengthen their fleets and fortify much of the eastern coast. Saxon ships, like the one above, had flat bottoms so that they could be rowed up shallow rivers for surprise attacks.

THE BLACK MONK
Legends tell that the 13th-century pirate Eustace the Monk had formed a pact with the devil and could make his ship invisible. But his magical powers did not help when he dabbled in politics. Leading an invasion fleet against England, Eustace was caught and beheaded at sea.

Geometric patterns of inlaid copper and silver

SPEAR-CATCHERS
A Viking trick that terrified opponents was to catch a spear in mid-flight, and hurl it straight back.

FACE TO FACE WITH PIRATES
For Viking warriors, glory in battle was everything and the ferocity of their attacks became legendary. The wild appearance of the bearded Norsemen fuelled their barbarous reputation. This fierce-looking Viking head was carved on the side of a wagon.

BROAD SWORD
Viking raiders attacked with broad, slashing swords.

Steering oar

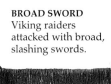

Handle of wood or bone has rotted away

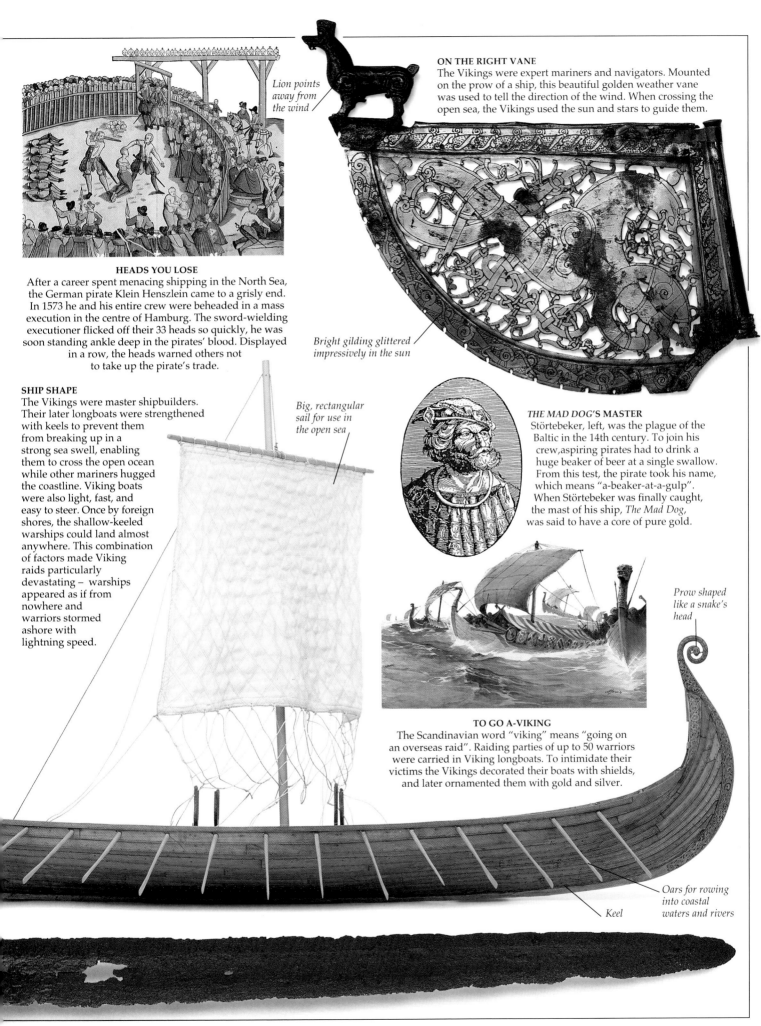

Lion points away from the wind

ON THE RIGHT VANE

The Vikings were expert mariners and navigators. Mounted on the prow of a ship, this beautiful golden weather vane was used to tell the direction of the wind. When crossing the open sea, the Vikings used the sun and stars to guide them.

HEADS YOU LOSE

After a career spent menacing shipping in the North Sea, the German pirate Klein Henszlein came to a grisly end. In 1573 he and his entire crew were beheaded in a mass execution in the centre of Hamburg. The sword-wielding executioner flicked off their 33 heads so quickly, he was soon standing ankle deep in the pirates' blood. Displayed in a row, the heads warned others not to take up the pirate's trade.

Bright gilding glittered impressively in the sun

SHIP SHAPE

The Vikings were master shipbuilders. Their later longboats were strengthened with keels to prevent them from breaking up in a strong sea swell, enabling them to cross the open ocean while other mariners hugged the coastline. Viking boats were also light, fast, and easy to steer. Once by foreign shores, the shallow-keeled warships could land almost anywhere. This combination of factors made Viking raids particularly devastating – warships appeared as if from nowhere and warriors stormed ashore with lightning speed.

Big, rectangular sail for use in the open sea

THE MAD DOG'S MASTER

Störtebeker, left, was the plague of the Baltic in the 14th century. To join his crew, aspiring pirates had to drink a huge beaker of beer at a single swallow. From this test, the pirate took his name, which means "a-beaker-at-a-gulp". When Störtebeker was finally caught, the mast of his ship, *The Mad Dog*, was said to have a core of pure gold.

Prow shaped like a snake's head

TO GO A-VIKING

The Scandinavian word "viking" means "going on an overseas raid". Raiding parties of up to 50 warriors were carried in Viking longboats. To intimidate their victims the Vikings decorated their boats with shields, and later ornamented them with gold and silver.

Oars for rowing into coastal waters and rivers

Keel

The Barbary coast

EUROPEAN CRUSADERS CALLED THEIR Muslim opponents "barbarians", so the Islamic sea rovers became known as Barbary (barbarian) corsairs. The Barbary corsairs first set sail from the southern coast of the Mediterranean, which became known as the Barbary coast. This was at the time of the Crusades, the holy wars between the Christians and Muslims that began at the end of the 11th century. In their sleek, fast galleys, the Barbary corsairs attacked trade vessels from Venice and Genoa in search of their preferred booty – men who could be sold as slaves. If corsairs boarded a Christian ship, the crew might be stripped of their clothes and belongings. Moments later, they would be taking the oars of the corsairs' ship, and changing course, for a life of slavery in an African port. In ferocious battles, they rammed ships bound for the Crusades, and captured the wealthy Christian knights on board. The most famous Barbary corsairs were feared throughout Europe. Their exploits made them heroes in the Islamic world.

THE BARBARY COAST

Muslim Arabs took over North Africa in the 7th century. The Barbarossas fought off the Spanish in the 16th century, leading to rule by the Turks. A "Dey" or "Bey" (local prince) controlled each city state. On this map, green represents the Christian-controlled area, beige the Muslim Ottoman empire.

North African coast, home of the first barbary corsairs

THE BARBAROSSA BROTHERS

Europeans nicknamed the two greatest Barbary pirates, Aruj and Kheir-ed-Din, "the Barbarossa Brothers" because of their red beards. Aruj was killed in 1518 but his brother led Muslim resistance to Spanish attacks so successfully that in 1530 he won the regency (command) of the city of Algiers. He died in 1546, greatly respected even by his enemies.

TURNING TURK

Sir Francis Verney (left) was one of a number of Europeans who "turned Turk" and joined the corsairs. Such men were welcomed because of their maritime skills. They paid taxes on their booty to the Barbary princes who protected them from revenge attacks in return. These Christian renegades sometimes adopted the Muslim faith of their new masters.

Verney's richly embroidered hat

Plush cloak was for everyday wear

Sleek Barbary galleys were capable of a speed of 9 knots (16 kmph/10 mph) over short distances

SEA BATTLE

The Barbary corsairs used slaves to power their sleek ships, but these men did not do any of the fighting. Muslim Janissaries – well-trained and highly disciplined professional soldiers – provided the military muscle. When a Barbary galley drew alongside its victim, as many as 100 Janissaries swarmed aboard the Christian vessel and overpowered the crew. This method of attack was very successful for the Barbary corsairs. Many Christian ships did not stand a chance.

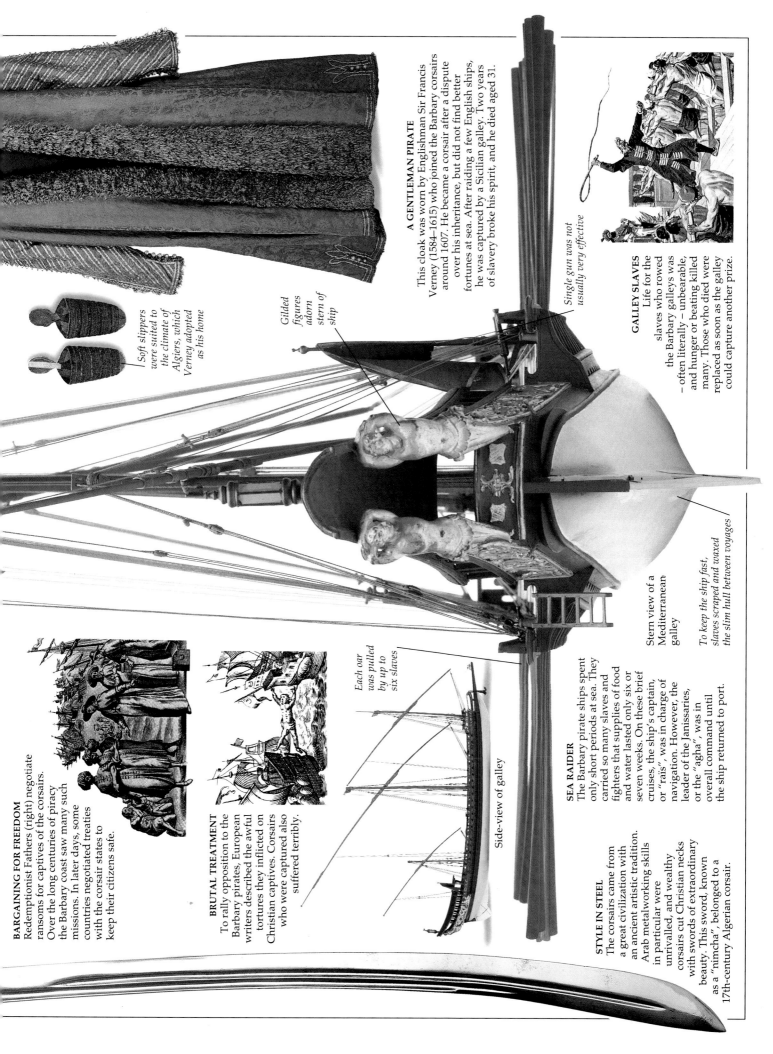

A GENTLEMAN PIRATE

This cloak was worn by Englishman Sir Francis Verney (1584–1615) who joined the Barbary corsairs around 1607. He became a corsair after a dispute over his inheritance, but did not find better fortunes at sea. After raiding a few English ships, he was captured by a Sicilian galley. Two years of slavery broke his spirit, and he died aged 31.

Soft slippers were suited to the climate of Algiers, which Verney adopted as his home

Gilded figures adorn stern of ship

Single gun was not usually very effective

GALLEY SLAVES

Life for the slaves who rowed the Barbary galleys was – often literally – unbearable, and hunger or beating killed many. Those who died were replaced as soon as the galley could capture another prize.

Stern view of a Mediterranean galley

To keep the ship fast, slaves scraped and waxed the slim hull between voyages

BARGAINING FOR FREEDOM

Redemptionist Fathers (right) negotiate ransoms for captives of the corsairs. Over the long centuries of piracy the Barbary coast saw many such missions. In later days, some countries negotiated treaties with the corsair states to keep their citizens safe.

BRUTAL TREATMENT

To rally opposition to the Barbary pirates, European writers described the awful tortures they inflicted on Christian captives. Corsairs who were captured also suffered terribly.

STYLE IN STEEL

The corsairs came from a great civilization with an ancient artistic tradition. Arab metalworking skills in particular were unrivalled, and wealthy corsairs cut Christian necks with swords of extraordinary beauty. This sword, known as a "nimcha", belonged to a 17th-century Algerian corsair.

Each oar was pulled by up to six slaves

Side-view of galley

SEA RAIDER

The Barbary pirate ships spent only short periods at sea. They carried so many slaves and fighters that supplies of food and water lasted only six or seven weeks. On these brief cruises, the ship's captain, or "raïs", was in charge of navigation. However, the leader of the Janissaries, or the "agha", was in overall command until the ship returned to port.

The corsairs of Malta

DRIVEN BY GOD AND BY GOLD, the corsairs of Malta led the fight against the Barbary pirates. With the Knights of Malta as their patrons, the corsairs waged a sea campaign against the "heathens" of Islam from their small island. When the Knights themselves captained the vessels, religious zeal was paramount, but as time went on, commerce crept in. The Knights still financed and organized the raids against their Barbary enemies, but for the Maltese, Corsicans, and French who crewed the galleys, the spoils of piracy became the main lure. The corsairs brought great wealth to Malta until the 1680s, when treaties between the European and Barbary powers led to a gradual decline in Mediterranean piracy.

EMBARKING FOR THE HOLY LAND
The Knights of the Order of St John were formed in the early years of the Crusades to defend Jerusalem, which the Christians held, against attacks by Islamic forces. This miniature shows Crusaders loading ships for the journey to the Holy Land. The Knights also created hospitals to care for the Crusaders.

A carrack, forerunner of the galleon

THE SIEGE OF MALTA
In 1565 the Knights of Malta had their greatest triumph against the Muslims when a fleet of the Ottoman Empire laid siege to Malta. The Knights were outnumbered five-to-one, but fought back bravely from inside their fort on Malta's north-east coast. When Spanish reinforcements arrived, the Ottoman fighters had to retreat. Six years later, the Knights fought again at the sea battle of Lepanto. Christian victory there finally ended Ottoman power in the Mediterranean.

A BOAT ON A BOTTLE
The Maltese galley fleet grew in size until the 1660s, when it numbered up to 30 carracks such as the one pictured on this pharmacy jar. At this time, the corsair trade employed as much as a third of the Maltese population.

CHRISTIAN GALLEY
The corsairs of Malta sailed similar galleys to their Muslim adversaries. However, the Christian galleys had two large sails instead of one, fewer oars, and more guns. The naked slaves at the oars were Muslims, and if anything they had a worse life than their counterparts at the oars of the Barbary galleys. A French officer observed that: "Many of the galley slaves have not room to sleep full length, for they put seven men on one bench [that is] ten feet long by four broad [3 m by 1.2 m]." This model represents a galley of the Knights of Malta c.1770, but the design had hardly changed since the 16th century.

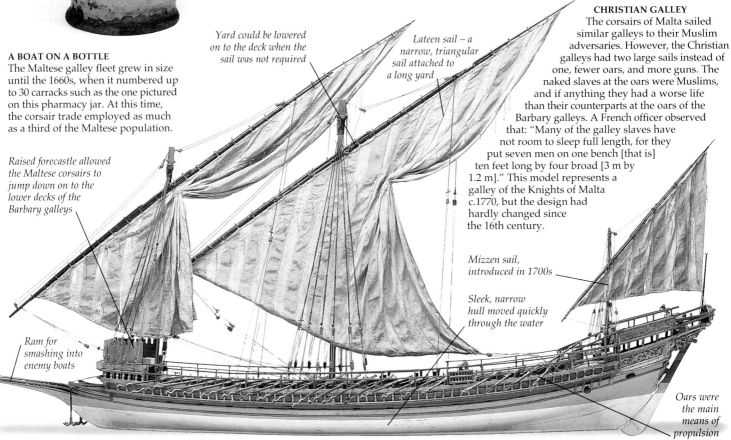

Yard could be lowered on to the deck when the sail was not required

Lateen sail – a narrow, triangular sail attached to a long yard

Raised forecastle allowed the Maltese corsairs to jump down on to the lower decks of the Barbary galleys

Ram for smashing into enemy boats

Mizzen sail, introduced in 1700s

Sleek, narrow hull moved quickly through the water

Oars were the main means of propulsion

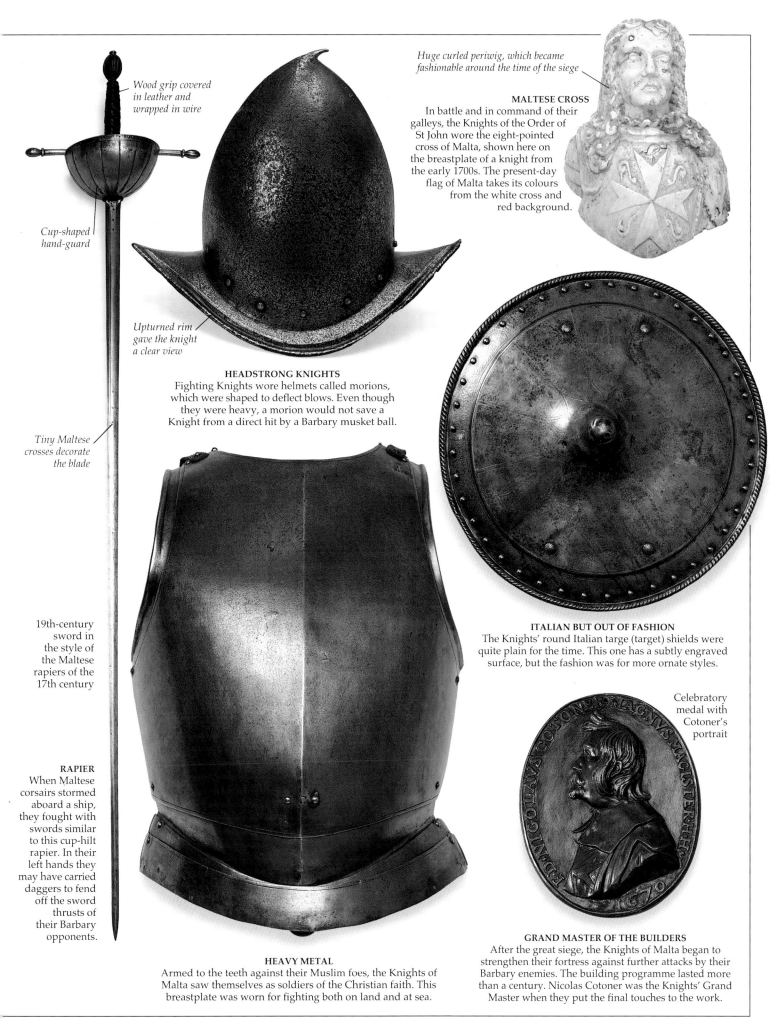

Wood grip covered in leather and wrapped in wire

Cup-shaped hand-guard

Tiny Maltese crosses decorate the blade

19th-century sword in the style of the Maltese rapiers of the 17th century

RAPIER
When Maltese corsairs stormed aboard a ship, they fought with swords similar to this cup-hilt rapier. In their left hands they may have carried daggers to fend off the sword thrusts of their Barbary opponents.

Upturned rim gave the knight a clear view

HEADSTRONG KNIGHTS
Fighting Knights wore helmets called morions, which were shaped to deflect blows. Even though they were heavy, a morion would not save a Knight from a direct hit by a Barbary musket ball.

Huge curled periwig, which became fashionable around the time of the siege

MALTESE CROSS
In battle and in command of their galleys, the Knights of the Order of St John wore the eight-pointed cross of Malta, shown here on the breastplate of a knight from the early 1700s. The present-day flag of Malta takes its colours from the white cross and red background.

ITALIAN BUT OUT OF FASHION
The Knights' round Italian targe (target) shields were quite plain for the time. This one has a subtly engraved surface, but the fashion was for more ornate styles.

Celebratory medal with Cotoner's portrait

HEAVY METAL
Armed to the teeth against their Muslim foes, the Knights of Malta saw themselves as soldiers of the Christian faith. This breastplate was worn for fighting both on land and at sea.

GRAND MASTER OF THE BUILDERS
After the great siege, the Knights of Malta began to strengthen their fortress against further attacks by their Barbary enemies. The building programme lasted more than a century. Nicolas Cotoner was the Knights' Grand Master when they put the final touches to the work.

The privateers

"KNOW YE THAT WE HAVE GRANTED and given license… to Adam Robernolt and William le Sauvage… to annoy our enemies at sea or by land… so that they shall share with us half of all their gain." With these words the English king Henry III issued one of the first letters of marque in 1243. Virtually a pirate's license, the letter was convenient for all concerned – the ship's crew were given the right to plunder without punishment, and the king acquired a free man-of-war (battleship) as well as a share of the booty. At first such ships were called "private men-of-war", but in the course of time they and their crews became known as privateers. Between the 16th and 18th centuries, privateering flourished as European nations fought each other in costly wars. Privateers were meant to attack only enemy shipping, but many found ways to bend the rules.

ROYAL HONOURS
The English queen Elizabeth I (1558–1603) honoured the adventurer and privateer Francis Drake (1540–1596), whom she called her "pirate", with a knighthood in 1581. Drake's privateering had brought her great wealth – more than £200,000 according to one estimate at the time.

OFFICIAL REPRISALS
English King Henry III (1216–1272), issued the first known letters of marque. There were two kinds. In wartime the king issued general letters of marque authorizing privateers to attack enemy shipping. In peacetime, merchants who had lost ships or cargoes to pirates could apply for a special letter of marque. This allowed them to attack shipping of the pirates' nation to recover their loss.

PRIVATEER PROMOTER
English navigator Walter Raleigh (1522–1618) was greatly in favour of privateering, recognizing that it brought a huge income to his country. He also promoted privateering for his own gain, equipping many privateers in the hope that he could finance a colony in Virginia, North America, on the proceeds.

THE PIRATES' LICENSE
Letters of marque, such as this one issued by England's king George III (1760–1820), contained many restrictions. But corrupt ship-owners could buy one, granting them license to plunder innocent merchant ships.

"HERE'S TO PLUNDER"
Prosperous privateer captains of the 18th century could afford to toast a new venture with fine glasses like this one. The engraving on the glass reads: "Success to the Duke of Cornwall Privateer."

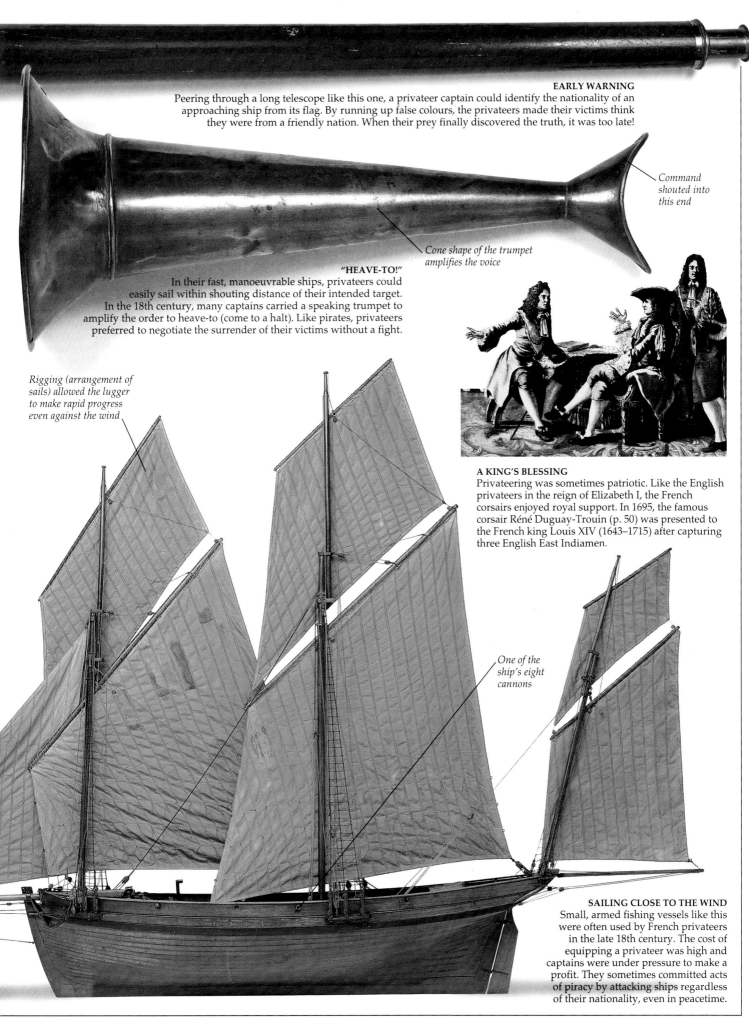

EARLY WARNING
Peering through a long telescope like this one, a privateer captain could identify the nationality of an approaching ship from its flag. By running up false colours, the privateers made their victims think they were from a friendly nation. When their prey finally discovered the truth, it was too late!

Command shouted into this end

Cone shape of the trumpet amplifies the voice

"HEAVE-TO!"
In their fast, manoeuvrable ships, privateers could easily sail within shouting distance of their intended target. In the 18th century, many captains carried a speaking trumpet to amplify the order to heave-to (come to a halt). Like pirates, privateers preferred to negotiate the surrender of their victims without a fight.

A KING'S BLESSING
Privateering was sometimes patriotic. Like the English privateers in the reign of Elizabeth I, the French corsairs enjoyed royal support. In 1695, the famous corsair Réné Duguay-Trouin (p. 50) was presented to the French king Louis XIV (1643–1715) after capturing three English East Indiamen.

Rigging (arrangement of sails) allowed the lugger to make rapid progress even against the wind

One of the ship's eight cannons

SAILING CLOSE TO THE WIND
Small, armed fishing vessels like this were often used by French privateers in the late 18th century. The cost of equipping a privateer was high and captains were under pressure to make a profit. They sometimes committed acts of piracy by attacking ships regardless of their nationality, even in peacetime.

The Spanish Main

A Spanish galleon

F AMED IN PIRATE LEGEND, the Spanish Main lured adventurers and pirates with the promise of untold riches. The Spanish Main was Spain's empire in the "New World" of North and South America. Discovered by Christopher Columbus in 1492, the New World contained treasures beyond the Europeans' wildest dreams. The Spanish conquistadors (conquerors) ruthlessly plundered the wealth of the Aztec and Inca nations of Mexico and Peru, and throughout the 16th and 17th centuries vast quantities of gold and silver were shipped back to Europe. The Spanish treasure ships soon attracted the attention of privateers and pirates eager for a share of the booty, signalling the beginning of piracy on the Spanish Main.

THE VOYAGES OF COLUMBUS
Seeking a western trade route to Asia, Italian-born navigator Christopher Columbus (1451–1506) arrived at the New World in 1492. He landed in the Bahamas on an island he called San Salvador, where he was welcomed by the local people, above. Columbus led four further Spanish expeditions to the New World and established the first permanent Spanish colony on the Caribbean island of Hispaniola (p. 27).

Aztec treasure loaded at Vera Cruz

Treasure ships rendezvous at Havana for return to Europe

Mexico

Atlantic Ocean

San Salvador

Cuba

Jamaica

Hispaniola

Pacific Ocean

Peru

Inca treasure loaded at Nombre de Dios

Panama

IN THE MAIN
The term "Spanish Main" originally meant the parts of the American mainland, from Mexico to Peru, taken by Spain. Later it came to include the islands and waters of the Caribbean.

High up in the crow's-nest, the ship's lookout kept watch for pirates

High forecastle (fo'c'sle)

Martin Behaim's 1491 globe has a gap where the Americas ought to be

OLD WORLD
Made before 1492, this globe leaves out the New World. It shows how Columbus thought he could reach Asia by crossing the Atlantic.

TREASURE SHIP
New World treasure was carried back to Europe in Spanish galleons. A galleon usually had a crew of about 200 men and an armament of up to 60 cannons. Although well built, with a strong wooden hull and powerful rig, these great ships were difficult to manoeuvre and in spite of their guns, galleons often proved no match for smaller, swifter pirate vessels. Therefore, as a safeguard, the treasure ships crossed the Atlantic in vast convoys of up to 100 vessels.

Equipped with a large, square sail on each main mast, a galleon sailed well with the wind behind it, but was slow towards the wind

AZTEC TREASURE
The solid gold jewellery of the Aztecs, such as this lip ornament, was exquisitely beautiful. However, the greedy Spaniards crushed or melted most of it down to save space on the treasure ships.

A well-armed galleon could outgun a pirate ship with cannon-fire, so pirates avoided direct confrontation, preferring to pick off the captain and crew with muskets

Tall, many-decked aftercastle increased wind resistance

Treasure chests were boarded up on lower decks and guarded by soldiers

Rudder

Hull floated high in the water, because the galleon had to load and unload in shallow rivers and bays

THE KINGDOM OF PERU
In 1529 conquistador Francisco Pizzaro (c.1476 –1541) led a small force to Peru. He easily captured the Inca king Atahualpa and ransomed him for the riches of his kingdom. The ransom arrived, but the Spanish killed Atahualpa anyway.

INCA GOLD
To ransom their king from Pizarro, the Inca people filled a room seven paces long and almost as wide with gold treasures like this figurine.

THE LAST KING
The Aztec king Quauhtemoc (c.1495–1525) surrendered to the Spanish conquistadors after a long fight. They treated him well at first, but later tortured and hanged him.

A NATION FALLS
This painting shows the Spanish army of Hernan Cortes (1485–1547) defeating the Aztecs in Mexico. In their lust for gold, the conquistadors completely destroyed the ancient American civilizations of the Aztecs and Incas.

New World privateers

SILVER SOURCE
The Spanish colonists at first enslaved local people to work the silver mines in the New World. But they proved unwilling – many died from beatings intended to drive them to work – so the Spanish brought in African slaves.

TREASURE FROM THE Spanish Main amazed the people of 16th-century Europe. The Spanish writer Bernal Díaz marvelled at items like a gold disc "in the shape of the sun, as big as a cartwheel". Soon Spain's many enemies were setting sail to get a share of the rich booty. Among the first on the scene were the French, and the English privateers, led by Drake and Hawkins, followed. Their spectacular success enouraged many adventurers to make trips to the Main. Desperate to return home rich, some crossed the thin line between privateering and piracy, attacking ships of any nation.

NARROWS NAVIGATOR
French ships made the first successful raids on the Spanish treasure galleons. Genoese navigator Giovanni da Verrazano (c.1485–c.1528), sailing for the French, took three Spanish ships in 1522. Two were laden with Mexican treasure and the third carried sugar, hides, and pearls. However, Verrazano is better known for the discovery of New York Bay in 1524.

ATTACKING A TREASURE SHIP
Treasure ships were most vulnerable to attack during the early stages of their voyage. Privateers knew the ships had to head north from the Caribbean to find a favourable wind before returning to Spain. Waiting off the American coast, the privateers could take the Spanish by surprise.

PIECES OF EIGHT
From New World gold and silver the Spanish minted doubloons and pieces of eight, which became the currency of later pirates.

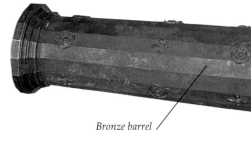

Bronze barrel

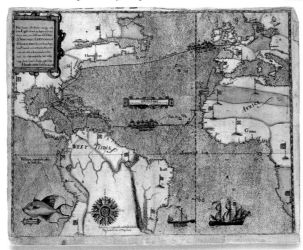

SAILING TO THE SPANISH MAIN
The exploits of English privateer and pirate Francis Drake (c.1540–96) made him a popular hero in his home country. The Spanish had attacked his ship in 1568, and the incident left him with a hatred for the nation. His 1585–86 voyage marked on the map above became known as Drake's "Descent on the Indies". He attacked Vigo in Spain, then crossed the Atlantic to raid the nation's colonies in the New World.

WARNING BEAT
Drake's successful defence of England against the Spanish Armada (invasion fleet) in 1588 further enhanced his reputation as a nautical hero. The drum he carried on board ship on his many voyages still exists, and is said to sound an eerie warning beat when England is in danger.

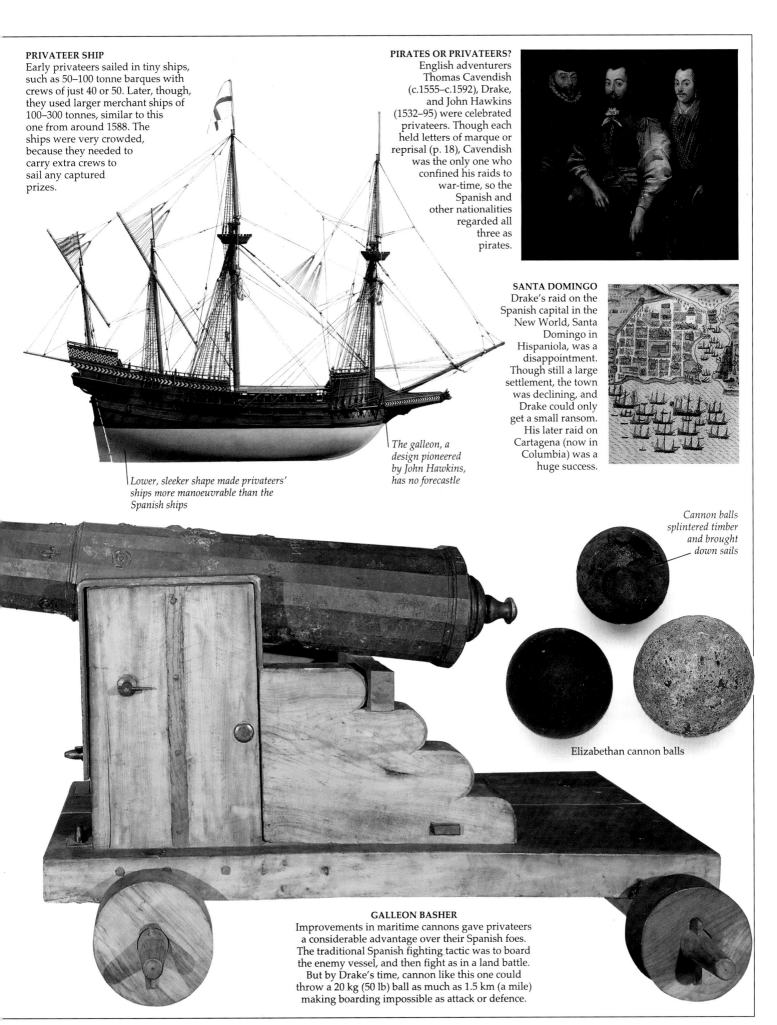

PRIVATEER SHIP
Early privateers sailed in tiny ships, such as 50–100 tonne barques with crews of just 40 or 50. Later, though, they used larger merchant ships of 100–300 tonnes, similar to this one from around 1588. The ships were very crowded, because they needed to carry extra crews to sail any captured prizes.

Lower, sleeker shape made privateers' ships more manoeuvrable than the Spanish ships

The galleon, a design pioneered by John Hawkins, has no forecastle

PIRATES OR PRIVATEERS?
English adventurers Thomas Cavendish (c.1555–c.1592), Drake, and John Hawkins (1532–95) were celebrated privateers. Though each held letters of marque or reprisal (p. 18), Cavendish was the only one who confined his raids to war-time, so the Spanish and other nationalities regarded all three as pirates.

SANTA DOMINGO
Drake's raid on the Spanish capital in the New World, Santa Domingo in Hispaniola, was a disappointment. Though still a large settlement, the town was declining, and Drake could only get a small ransom. His later raid on Cartagena (now in Columbia) was a huge success.

Cannon balls splintered timber and brought down sails

Elizabethan cannon balls

GALLEON BASHER
Improvements in maritime cannons gave privateers a considerable advantage over their Spanish foes. The traditional Spanish fighting tactic was to board the enemy vessel, and then fight as in a land battle. But by Drake's time, cannon like this one could throw a 20 kg (50 lb) ball as much as 1.5 km (a mile) making boarding impossible as attack or defence.

Navigation and maps

PIRATICAL SUCCESS on the Spanish Main (p. 20) meant outwitting, out-sailing, and out-fighting the chosen quarry, but how did pirates find their victims? Navigation was primitive. Pirates had to position their ships along the routes taken by Spanish treasure ships using a mixture of knowledge, common sense, and good luck. They could estimate latitude quite accurately by measuring the position of the sun, but judging longitude was more difficult. Apart from a compass, the most vital navigational aid available to a pirate captain was a chart. Spanish ships had surveyed much of the "New World" coast in the early 16th century, and their detailed charts were valuable prizes. With a stolen Spanish chart, pirates and buccaneers could plunder the riches of new areas of coastline.

This page of the waggoner shows the coastline around Panama

Dividers and chart

Vellum chart

Cross-staff

Globe

Astrolabe

SEA ARTISTS AT WORK
Pirates called skilled navigators "sea artists"; this fanciful illustration shows a group of them with the tools of their trade. In ideal conditions they could judge distance to within about 2 km (1.3 miles), but on the deck of a pitching ship navigation was far less precise.

A WAGGONER OF THE SOUTH SEA
Pirates called books of charts "waggoners". This waggoner of the Pacific coast of South America was seized from the Spanish by the buccaneer Bartholomew Sharp. In 1681 he wrote in his journal: "I took a Spanish manuscript of prodigious value – it describes all the ports, roads, harbours, bays, sands, rocks and rising of the land, and instructions how to work a ship into any port or harbour." English map-maker William Hack made this copy in 1685.

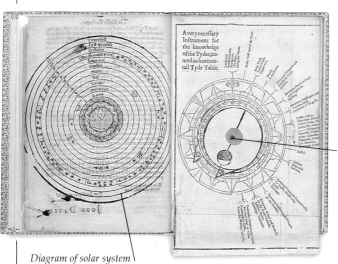

Diagram of solar system

A volvelle, or moving diagram, for calculating the tides from the phase of the moon

SECRETS OF THE SEA
English navigator John Davis (c.1550–1605) gathered some of his wide knowledge of the sea when he sailed with the privateer Thomas Cavendish in 1591. His book *The Seaman's Secrets*, above, summed up much of what he knew, and was essential reading for pirate pilots. This ingenious volvelle shows the position of the moon and tides with the aid of moving circular templates.

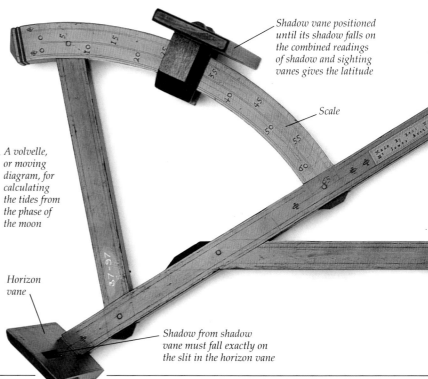

Shadow vane positioned until its shadow falls on the combined readings of shadow and sighting vanes gives the latitude

Scale

Horizon vane

Shadow from shadow vane must fall exactly on the slit in the horizon vane

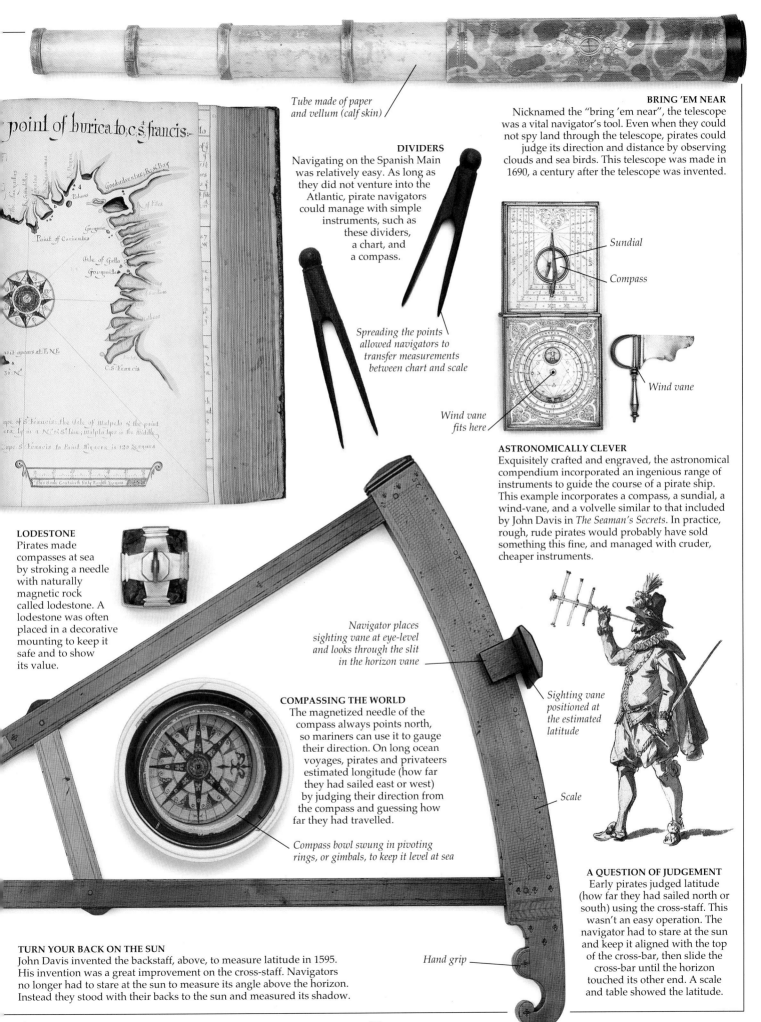

Tube made of paper and vellum (calf skin)

BRING 'EM NEAR
Nicknamed the "bring 'em near", the telescope was a vital navigator's tool. Even when they could not spy land through the telescope, pirates could judge its direction and distance by observing clouds and sea birds. This telescope was made in 1690, a century after the telescope was invented.

DIVIDERS
Navigating on the Spanish Main was relatively easy. As long as they did not venture into the Atlantic, pirate navigators could manage with simple instruments, such as these dividers, a chart, and a compass.

Spreading the points allowed navigators to transfer measurements between chart and scale

Sundial

Compass

Wind vane

Wind vane fits here

ASTRONOMICALLY CLEVER
Exquisitely crafted and engraved, the astronomical compendium incorporated an ingenious range of instruments to guide the course of a pirate ship. This example incorporates a compass, a sundial, a wind-vane, and a volvelle similar to that included by John Davis in *The Seaman's Secrets*. In practice, rough, rude pirates would probably have sold something this fine, and managed with cruder, cheaper instruments.

LODESTONE
Pirates made compasses at sea by stroking a needle with naturally magnetic rock called lodestone. A lodestone was often placed in a decorative mounting to keep it safe and to show its value.

Navigator places sighting vane at eye-level and looks through the slit in the horizon vane

Sighting vane positioned at the estimated latitude

COMPASSING THE WORLD
The magnetized needle of the compass always points north, so mariners can use it to gauge their direction. On long ocean voyages, pirates and privateers estimated longitude (how far they had sailed east or west) by judging their direction from the compass and guessing how far they had travelled.

Scale

Compass bowl swung in pivoting rings, or gimbals, to keep it level at sea

A QUESTION OF JUDGEMENT
Early pirates judged latitude (how far they had sailed north or south) using the cross-staff. This wasn't an easy operation. The navigator had to stare at the sun and keep it aligned with the top of the cross-bar, then slide the cross-bar until the horizon touched its other end. A scale and table showed the latitude.

TURN YOUR BACK ON THE SUN
John Davis invented the backstaff, above, to measure latitude in 1595. His invention was a great improvement on the cross-staff. Navigators no longer had to stare at the sun to measure its angle above the horizon. Instead they stood with their backs to the sun and measured its shadow.

Hand grip

The buccaneers

ENGLAND'S KING, James I, opened a bloody chapter in the history of the Spanish Main (p. 20) in 1603. To end the chaos of privateering raids in the Caribbean, he withdrew all letters of marque (p. 18). This had disastrous consequences. Bands of lawless buccaneers soon replaced the privateers. Originally hunters from the island of Hispaniola, the buccaneers banded together into a loyal brotherhood when the hated Spanish tried to drive them out. They began by attacking small Spanish ships, then went after bigger prizes. Convicts, outlaws, and escaped slaves swelled their numbers. The buccaneers obeyed no laws except their own, and their leaders maintained discipline with horrible acts of cruelty. However, some, such as Henry Morgan, fought for fame and glory and became heroes.

BLOODY BUCCANEERS
The original buccaneers lived by supplying meat, fat, and hides to passing ships. They hunted pigs and cattle which had bred rapidly when Spanish settlers left the island of Hispaniola. Buccaneers had a wild reputation. They dressed in uncured hides, and were stinking and bloody from their trade.

AN EARLY BARBECUE
The Arawak Indians taught the buccaneers how to cure meat in smokehouses like this one. These "boucans" gave the "boucaniers" their name.

A BUCCANEERING JOURNAL
Surgeon Basil Ringrose (1653–86) sailed with the buccaneer Bartholomew Sharp on his expedition of 1680–82 along the Pacific coast of South America. His detailed journal of the voyage is one of the main sources of knowledge of buccaneering life.

Tortuga

Isle à Vache

17th-century mariner's chart of Hispaniola (present-day Haiti)

CRUEL AND BLOODTHIRSTY CUTTHROATS
In the dangerous waters of the Spanish Main, life was cheap and the torture of prisoners commonplace. Nevertheless, the cruelty of the buccaneers became legendary. L'Ollonais, above, tortured his victims with grisly originality. On one occasion he cut out the heart of a Spanish prisoner and stuffed it into the mouth of another.

Sword and sheath reputedly carried by one of Morgan's buccaneers in 1670

FRANCIS L'OLLONAIS

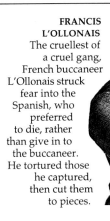

The cruellest of a cruel gang, French buccaneer L'Ollonais struck fear into the Spanish, who preferred to die, rather than give in to the buccaneer. He tortured those he captured, then cut them to pieces.

ROCK BRAZILIANO

Nicknamed for his long exile in Brazil, this "brutish and foolish" drunkard loathed the Spanish. He once spit-roasted two Spanish farmers alive because they would not give him their pigs for food.

BARTHOLOMEW PORTUGUES

Ingenious and daring, Bartholomew Portugues captured valuable prizes – and lost his fortunes a few days later. Though he could not swim, he escaped from a prison ship by splashing ashore using wine jars for floats.

Chart mounted on hinged oak "platts" to protect it at sea

HISPANOLA

Saona

SIR HENRY MORGAN

The most famous of the buccaneers, Welshman Henry Morgan (1635?–88) was a natural leader. He was probably just as cruel as other buccaneers, but his daring attacks on Spanish colonies, most notably Panama, won him an English knighthood and governorship of Jamaica.

THE BUCCANEER ISLAND

As hunters, the buccaneers lived peacefully on Hispaniola, left, until the Spanish attacked them and destroyed the animals they lived on. They formed the "Brotherhood of the Coast" to defend themselves, and some buccaneers moved to Tortuga, where they could prey easily on Spanish ships. The arrival of French garrisons later dispersed some of the brotherhood to Île à Vache and Saona.

THE ORIGIN OF THE CUTLASS

According to legend, buccaneers invented the cutlass. The long knives used by the original buccaneers to butcher meat for the boucan evolved into the famous short sword used by all seamen.

A BRUTAL ATTACK

Morgan carried out his raids on Spanish colonies with military discipline, but without mercy. In 1668 his 800 men defeated the soldiers of El Puerto del Principe on Cuba, right. They forced the men of the town to surrender by threatening to tear their wives and children to pieces. Imprisoned in churches, the people starved while the buccaneers pillaged their possessions.

Weapons

Boom! WITH A DEAFENING EXPLOSION and a puff of smoke, a pirate cannon signals the attack. Crack! A well-aimed musket ball catches the helmsman, but the ship careers on, out of control. Crash! The mainsail tumbles to the deck as the boarding pirates chop through the sail lifts. After such a dramatic show of force, most sailors were reluctant to challenge the pirates who rushed on board, bristling with weapons and yelling terrifying threats. Few crews put up a fight. Those who did faced the razor-sharp cutlasses of seasoned cutthroats. The only way to repel a pirate attack successfully was to avoid a pitched battle. Brave crew members barricaded themselves into the strongest part of the ship, and fought back courageously with guns and also home-made bombs.

FLYING CANNON BALLS
Cannons rarely sank a ship, but inside the hull the impact of the iron balls created a whirlwind of deadly wooden splinters. Chain-shot (two balls chained together and aimed high) took down the masts and sails to disable a vessel.

CUTTHROAT CUTLASS
In the 17th and 18th centuries, the cutlass was favoured by all fighting men at sea. Its short, broad blade was the ideal weapon for hand-to-hand fighting on board ship – a longer sword would be easily tangled in the rigging.

Short blade was easy to wield on a crowded deck

Firing mechanism, or lock

Wooden stock

MUSKETOON
The short barrel of the musketoon limited its accuracy, so pirates would have used this gun only when they were close to their victims. Like the longer musket, it was fired from the shoulder, but the short barrel made the musketoon easier to handle on a cramped, pitching deck on the high seas.

Patch and musket ball

Patchboxes were often fixed to a belt

PATCHBOXES
To stop a musket ball from rolling out of a loaded gun, pirates wrapped the ball in a patch of cloth to make it fit tightly in the barrel. Patches were stored in patchboxes.

Frizzen

Cock holds flint, which strikes frizzen, making sparks

Sparks ignite powder in priming pan

FLINTLOCK PISTOL
Light and portable, the pistol was the pirate's favourite weapon for boarding. However, sea air sometimes dampened the powder, so that the gun misfired and went off with a quiet "flash in the pan". Re-loading was so slow that pirates often didn't bother, preferring to use the gun's hard butt as a club.

Brass-covered butt could be used as a club

Ramrod for pushing the ball and patch into the barrel

Cock

Flint

MARKSMAN'S MUSKET
With a long musket, a pirate marksman could take out the helmsman of a ship from a distance. Rifling, or spiral grooving cut inside the musket barrel, spun the musket ball so that it flew in a straight line. This improved accuracy, but a marksman needed calm seas for careful aiming.

Trigger

Trigger-guard

Butt rests against the shoulder

WHIRLING CUTLASSES

In the battle to capture Blackbeard (pp. 30–31), the pirate captain and his crew were so injured from the slashing of the whirling cutlasses that "the sea was tinctured [stained] with blood round the vessel".

AXE ATTACK

Pirates boarding a large vessel used axes to help climb its high wooden sides. Once on deck, their axes brought down the sails – a single blow cut through ropes as thick as a man's arm.

NO QUARTER

If pirates' victims resisted attack, none of them would be spared in the fight that followed. Though this 19th-century print possibly exaggerates the cold-blooded brutality of the pirates, even women received no quarter (mercy).

COMING ABOARD!

The notorious Barbary corsair, Dragut Rais, right, had a reputation as a brave fighter. Here, he is storming aboard a ship armed with the pirates' favoured weapons: pistols, short sword, and axe.

Muzzle

Brass barrel

DAGGERS DRAWN

The dagger was small enough for a pirate to conceal under clothes in a surprise attack, and was lethal on the lower deck where there was no space to swing a sword.

FIGHT TO THE DEATH

Battles between Mediterranean pirates in the 16th and 17th centuries were especially ferocious, because they pitted two great religions against each other. Christian forces – Greek corsairs in this picture – fought not just for booty, but also because they believed they had God on their side. Their Ottoman opponents were Muslims, and believed the same. This 19th century engraving vividly captures the no-holds-barred nature of their conflict.

GREAT BALLS OF FIRE

Thrown from the high fo'c'sle of a pirate ship, a home-made grenade could start a fire that spread quickly. More often, a smouldering mixture of tar and rags filled the bomb, creating a smoke screen of confusion and panic.

BAREFOOT BARBS

French corsairs sometimes tossed these vicious-looking caltrops or crowsfeet onto the deck of a ship they were boarding. Since sailors worked barefoot to avoid slipping on wet decks, the spikes could inflict terrible injuries if trodden on.

Spikes angled so that one always points up

BIG GUNS

Firing cannon effectively required rigid discipline: even the best drilled navy gun teams needed two to five minutes to load and fire. Ill-disciplined pirate crews rarely managed more than one shot per gun before boarding.

Pirates of the Caribbean

HE WAS A STORY-BOOK PIRATE, with wild, staring eyes and a cruel streak; he wore lighted fuses in his hair, drank rum mixed with gunpowder, and twisted his huge black beard around his ears to make his appearance more alarming. Was it surprising that Blackbeard terrified 18th-century mariners, and even his own crew? Blackbeard was typical of a new breed of pirate who succeeded the buccaneers. During the 17th century some Caribbean islands had welcomed the buccaneers, but when they became increasingly unruly, they were driven from their strongholds. Many of the buccaneers found work as privateers during the wars of the early 18th century. But when peace returned, the pirate ways of freedom and adventure still beckoned. Most crews returned to plain piracy, plundering shipping of every flag and leaving a trail of terror behind them. New pirate ports blossomed in the Bahamas, and on mainland America.

Edward Low used his cutlass with awesome skill to slaughter the crew of a Spanish man-of-war in 1723

Large-buckled shoes, fashionable in the early 18th century

BULLY BOYS
Low's men could be as cruel as their captain. This picture shows one of Low's men shooting a Spanish prisoner at point blank range.

CRUEL COWARD
18th-century English captain Edward Low had a reputation as one of the cruellest pirates: he was said to have cut off a man's lips, and fried them in front of him; he cut off the ears of another, and made his victim eat them with salt and pepper. But another account suggests that he had a soft spot, and often wept for his orphan son in Boston.

Pirates raised a square sail on this mainmast when the wind was behind the ship

Versatile ketch rig could sail in almost any direction except directly into the wind

Bowsprit could be almost as long as the hull

SWIFT SLOOP
American and Bahamian pirates cruised mainly on inshore waters, so they did not need large ocean-going ships. Instead they chose small ketches or sloops like this one. With several triangular sails set on a long bowsprit, these ships were very fast, and they could also rig a square sail in order to make the most of a following wind.

Planks of hull butted tightly together (rather than overlapping) to reduce friction in the water

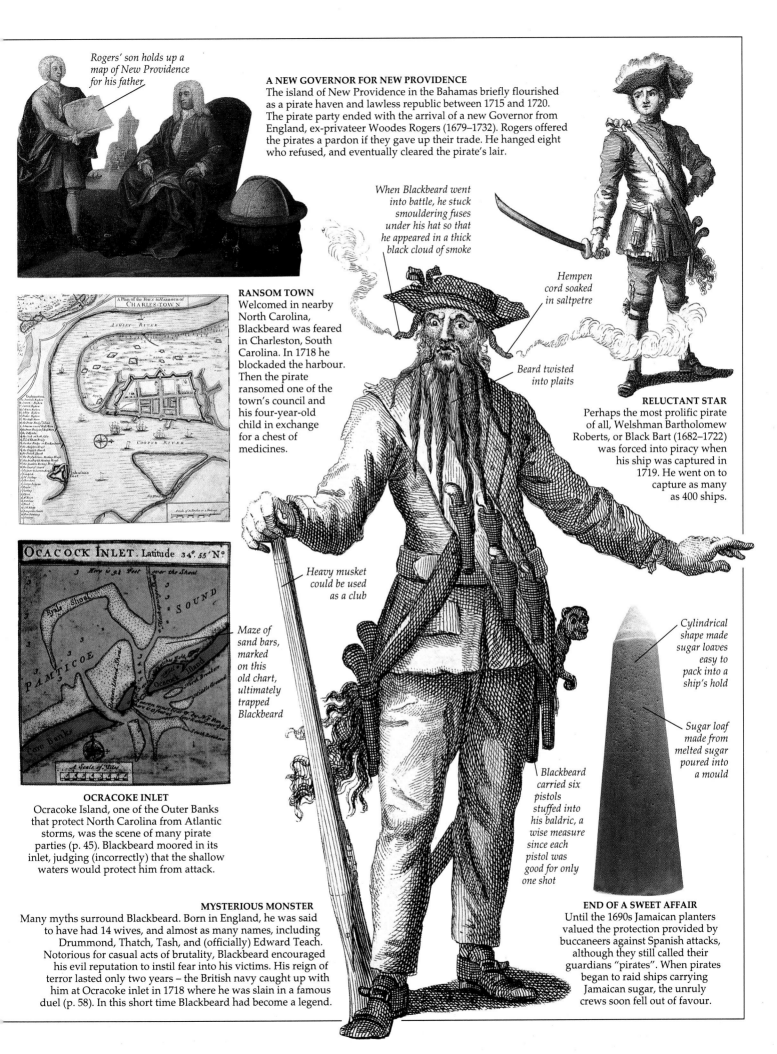

Rogers' son holds up a map of New Providence for his father

A NEW GOVERNOR FOR NEW PROVIDENCE
The island of New Providence in the Bahamas briefly flourished as a pirate haven and lawless republic between 1715 and 1720. The pirate party ended with the arrival of a new Governor from England, ex-privateer Woodes Rogers (1679–1732). Rogers offered the pirates a pardon if they gave up their trade. He hanged eight who refused, and eventually cleared the pirate's lair.

When Blackbeard went into battle, he stuck smouldering fuses under his hat so that he appeared in a thick black cloud of smoke

Hempen cord soaked in saltpetre

Beard twisted into plaits

RANSOM TOWN
Welcomed in nearby North Carolina, Blackbeard was feared in Charleston, South Carolina. In 1718 he blockaded the harbour. Then the pirate ransomed one of the town's council and his four-year-old child in exchange for a chest of medicines.

RELUCTANT STAR
Perhaps the most prolific pirate of all, Welshman Bartholomew Roberts, or Black Bart (1682–1722) was forced into piracy when his ship was captured in 1719. He went on to capture as many as 400 ships.

Heavy musket could be used as a club

Maze of sand bars, marked on this old chart, ultimately trapped Blackbeard

Cylindrical shape made sugar loaves easy to pack into a ship's hold

Sugar loaf made from melted sugar poured into a mould

Blackbeard carried six pistols stuffed into his baldric, a wise measure since each pistol was good for only one shot

OCRACOKE INLET
Ocracoke Island, one of the Outer Banks that protect North Carolina from Atlantic storms, was the scene of many pirate parties (p. 45). Blackbeard moored in its inlet, judging (incorrectly) that the shallow waters would protect him from attack.

MYSTERIOUS MONSTER
Many myths surround Blackbeard. Born in England, he was said to have had 14 wives, and almost as many names, including Drummond, Thatch, Tash, and (officially) Edward Teach. Notorious for casual acts of brutality, Blackbeard encouraged his evil reputation to instil fear into his victims. His reign of terror lasted only two years – the British navy caught up with him at Ocracoke inlet in 1718 where he was slain in a famous duel (p. 58). In this short time Blackbeard had become a legend.

END OF A SWEET AFFAIR
Until the 1690s Jamaican planters valued the protection provided by buccaneers against Spanish attacks, although they still called their guardians "pirates". When pirates began to raid ships carrying Jamaican sugar, the unruly crews soon fell out of favour.

Women pirates

PIRACY WAS A MAN'S WORLD, just like the 18th-century worlds of business, art, or politics. So women who dreamed of sailing the seas under the Jolly Roger had to become men, or at least to dress, fight, drink, and swear like men. Those who succeeded escaped the notice of history – today we know only of those who were unmasked. The bold exploits of female pirates Mary Read and Anne Bonny seem amazing, but they are not surprising. They form part of a long tradition of women adventurers who dressed as men to get equal treatment. Like many of their female contemporaries, Read and Bonny lacked neither strength nor courage. Fighting fearlessly alongside each other in battle, this formidable duo daunted even the bravest of pirates and naval men.

MARY READ
English pirate Mary Read (1690–1720) found it easier to make her way in life dressed as a man. She fought in the English army and navy – disguised in men's clothes – and when Rackham's pirates captured her transatlantic ship, she joined them. Read's valour shamed the pirates she sailed with. During an attack all but one hid while she and Anne Bonny fought. When they would not come out and "fight like men", Read shot the cowards.

THE TERRIBLE ALVILDA
One of the first female pirate captains was Alvilda, a Goth who came from southern Sweden, in the time before the Vikings. She went to sea with an all-woman crew to avoid an enforced marriage to Danish Prince Alf.

A CUTLASS ABOVE THE REST
When he threatened her lover, Mary Read challenged a fellow pirate to a duel. She easily despatched her foe by running him through with her cutlass.

CALICO JACK
From 1718 "Calico" Jack Rackham, left, and Anne Bonny were pirates and lovers in the Caribbean, later joined by Mary Read. All three were caught when Rackham's ship was surprised by a British navy sloop off Jamaica. Bonny and Read were the only members of the intoxicated crew brave enough to fend off the attack, but they were soon captured. In 1720 the pirates were sentenced to death. As Rackham went to the gallows, Bonny told him: "Had you fought like a man, you need not have been hanged like a dog"!

Dashing red sash favoured by pirates

PIRATE DRESS
Women were banned from most pirate ships, so Mary Read and Anne Bonny had to disguise themselves in clothes like these. Descriptions of the women's attire differ: one writer claimed they hid their identities from the crew up to the moment of their trial. But other eyewitnesses said that they wore men's clothes only for fighting.

Buckled leather shoe fashionable in the 18th-century

Hard-wearing calico trousers with bone buttons

A BRILLIANT DISGUISE?
The loose-fitting cut of the pirate jacket, below, fooled fellow pirates, but it couldn't completely conceal the feminine shapes of Read and Bonny from the sharp eyes of another woman. When they attacked a merchant ship, female passenger Dorothy Thomas recalled: "By the largeness of their breasts, I believed them to be women."

WIELDING AN AXE
Portraits of Anne Bonny and Mary Read show them armed with hefty boarding axes like this one. The fact that they could swing these heavy tools suggests they had the strength to tackle any task on board ship.

Linen cravat to keep the neck warm

Loose-fitting blue jacket

Turban-like headgear worn by pirates and other seafarers

Pirate queen Ching Shih battles with dagger and cutlass

Leather warrior's belt, or baldric, for holding a cutlass

CHING SHIH
In the early 19th century, a huge pirate fleet terrorized the China Sea. Its commander was the brilliant female pirate Ching Shih. Female sea captains weren't unusual, but the vastness of Ching Shih's empire was – she controlled 1,800 ships and about 80,000 pirates.

Blue-and-white checked sailor's shirt made of linen

DAGGERS DRAWN
Charlotte de Berry's life as a pirate began when she led a mutiny against a cruel captain who had assaulted her. She cut off the captain's head with a sharp dagger.

Flintlock pistol

CHARLOTTE DE BERRY
Born in England in 1636, Charlotte de Berry, right, grew up dreaming of a life at sea. Dressed as a man she followed her husband into the navy. Later, forced aboard an Africa-bound vessel, Charlotte led a mutiny and took over the ship. Under her command, the crew turned pirates and cruised the African coast capturing gold ships.

ANNE BONNY
When Anne Bonny, right, met the pirate Jack Rackham, she left her sailor husband to take up a life of piracy dressed as a man. Bonny accidentally fell in love with Mary Read when Read, also in male disguise, joined Rackham's crew. Read told Bonny her secret and the pair became firm friends. When Rackham's pirates were captured, the two women escaped the death penalty since both were pregnant.

The Jolly Roger

GRAVE EXAMPLE
Pirates probably borrowed their symbols from gravestones, like this 18th-century example from Scotland.

Emblazoned with emblems of death, the Jolly Roger warned pirates' victims to surrender without a fight. Although it filled mariners with dread, it was less feared than a plain red flag, which signalled death to all who saw it. This bloody banner meant the pirates would give no quarter (mercy) in the ensuing battle. But the threatening Jolly Roger usually served its purpose. Some crews defended their ship bravely, but often sailors were keen to surrender, sometimes opting to join the pirates. Worked to death and close to mutiny anyway, many sailors saw piracy as a life of freedom, and perhaps wealth, with only a slim chance of being caught.

A LEGEND IN THE MAKING
The flag of Henry Avery (p. 47) closely resembles the skull-and-crossbones-style Jolly Roger of pirate legend. In the 1600s the skull-and-crossbones was commonly used to represent death and it was adopted by pirates towards the end of the century. However, the skull-and-crossbones was not a standard pirate emblem; every pirate had his own particular Jolly Roger design.

A SCIMITAR TOO FAR
The sword has always been a symbol of power, so the message of Thomas Tew's (p. 47) flag was plain to all. However, the choice of the curved Asian scimitar was an unfortunate one for Tew, for it may have been a similar sword that slew him in the battle for the Indian ship *Futteh Mahmood* in 1695.

TIME FLIES
The hour-glass appears on many pirate flags. On pirate Christopher Moody's (1694–1722) flag, as on many gravestones of the age, the glass had wings to show how rapidly the sand was running out. A traditional symbol of death, the hour-glass warned sailors that the time for surrender was limited.

Not all pirate flags were black and white

A PIRATE SEAMSTRESS
Jolly Rogers were rough and ready affairs, run up by a pirate ship's sailmaker or any member of the crew who was handy with a needle. New Providence pirates had flags made for them by a sailmaker's widow who accepted payment in brandy.

Pirates pretend to be female passengers to deceive an approaching ship

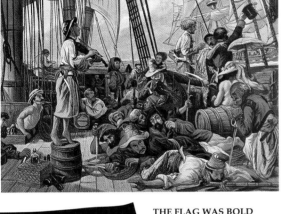

MASTERS OF DECEPTION
Pirates would have probably come off worst in a conventional naval battle, so they often relied on deception and terror to trap their prey. When approaching a target pirates sometimes flew a friendly flag, then at the last minute they raised Jolly Roger to terrify their victims into surrendering without a fight. If this failed, they launched a surprise attack, boarded the ship and overpowered the crew.

THE FLAG WAS BOLD
Women pirates Mary Read and Anne Bonny (pp. 32–33) probably fought under this emblem of a skull and crossed swords. It was the flag flown by their pirate captain Jack Rackham (p. 32). However, Rackham wasn't as bold as his flag suggested. When the British navy attacked his ship, he hid in the hold with the rest of his drunken men, leaving the two women to fight alone.

BLOODY BLACKBEARD
Blackbeard's (p. 30) flag shows a devil-like skeleton holding an hour-glass, an arrow, and a bleeding heart. The Jolly Roger may have been named after the devil – Old Roger – but it probably got its name from the French term for the red flag – "Jolie Rouge".

FORTUNE FAVOURS THE FAST
Pirate ships and those of their victims varied widely, so there was no single method of attack. However, pirates usually had no trouble overtaking their quarry, because they generally favoured small, fast ships; the merchant ships they preyed on were more heavily built, slowed by heavy cargo.

DRINKING WITH DEATH
Drinking with a skeleton, Bartholomew Roberts (p. 39) toasted death on his flag. He also flew a second flag, which showed him astride two skulls, labelled ABH and AMH. The initials stood for "A Barbadian's Head" and "A Martinican's Head" – a vow of revenge against two Caribbean islands that dared cross him.

Pirate treasure

WHEN PIRATES SWARMED ABOARD a heavily laden ship, they hoped to find a hold full of gold. If they were lucky, the prize could make the entire crew wealthy beyond their wildest dreams. When Thomas Tew (p. 47) raided a ship in the Indian Ocean in 1693, every member of the ship's crew received a share worth £3,000, and by the standards of the time, all became millionaires (an English naval seaman then earned £1 a month). Such rich prizes were exceptional. More often, the pirate crew shared out much more modest treasures or, worse, discovered a hold full of a bulky cargo.

Rose-sapphire pendant cross

SWAGGER DAGGER
When the cargo was not worth plundering, the pirates contented themselves with robbing the passengers and stealing their valuables. An elaborate dagger like this one was too good for fighting, but it would fetch a fine price.

X MARKS THE SPOT
Buried hoards of pirate treasure are mostly romantic myths, although William Kidd (p. 46), right, did bury treasure, at Gardiner's Island, just off the eastern tip of Long Island, New York. It was all recovered.

Emerald salamander

Bloodstone reliquary

Garnet fan-holder

Rose sapphire

Malachite

Rose-sapphire cross

"Piece-of-eight" or Spanish peso

Gold doubloon

SPANISH GOLD
Pirates' favourite booty was Spanish gold or silver. A Spanish gold doubloon was worth about seven weeks' pay for an ordinary sailor. Silver "pieces-of-eight" could be cut into pieces to make small change.

Pirates would have forced the lid of this multiple-lock strong box

Late-16th-century English money chest

Gold seal ring

Ruby

Enamelled cross

Garnet

Amethyst

Large ruby

JEWELS TO DIE FOR
Dividing a cargo of precious gems fairly wasn't always easy. John Taylor's raid on a Portuguese East Indiaman in 1721 rewarded each of his crew with £4,000 and 42 small diamonds. One crewman was given a single large diamond instead of 42 little ones; unhappy with his share, he broke it into smaller pieces with a hammer!

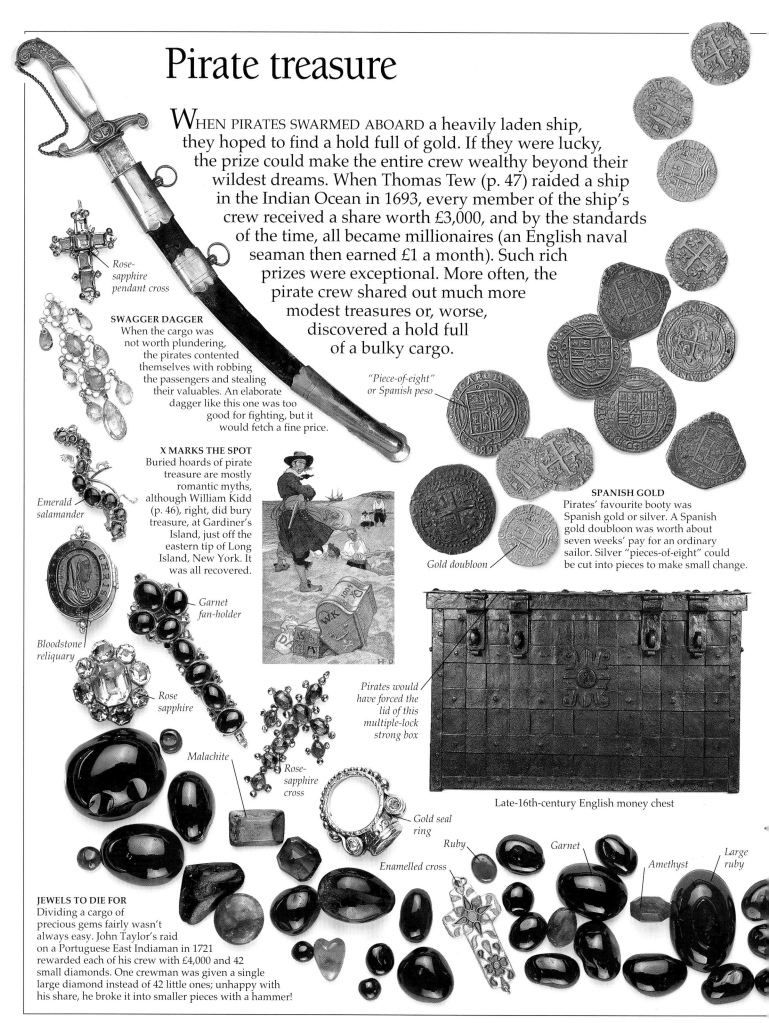

SHARING OUT THE SPOILS

Pirates divided up a haul more or less equally, although the captain and other "officers" usually received more than others. The carpenter sometimes got less, because he did not risk his life in the attack. Under one typical scheme, the captain received 2.5 times as much as a seaman, the surgeon 1.25 times, but the carpenter got just three quarters of a share. Boys got a half share.

WELL WORTH ITS WEIGHT

In this illustration, right, Henry Avery (p. 47) and his crew are loading heavy treasure chests from the captured Arab ship *Gang-i-Sawai*. Avery's haul on this occasion was reputed to be around £325,000. Each member of his crew received £2,000, and Avery himself was able to retire from piracy on the proceeds.

17th-century diamond and amethyst necklace

PRIZE POSSESSION

When privateers boarded a ship, they were supposed to return to their home port before dividing the cargo. However, the crew were often entitled to "pillage", which meant they could steal the personal possessions of passengers and crew, such as this expensive necklace.

Tiger's eye

Sapphire

Ruby

Rubies

PRECIOUS PISTOL

Weapons and ammunition were highly prized booty among pirates.

TEMPTING TRINKETS

Privateers were meant to share out pillaged goods according to rank, but, in practice, many of them just pocketed small items such as these gold rings.

LIFE-SAVING LOOT

Pirates often relied on stealing everyday necessities from their victims. Food and medicine were usually in short supply. One victim of pirates in 1720 reported that: "No part of the cargo was so much valued by the robbers as the doctor's chest, for they were all poxed to a great degree."

18th-century ship's medicine chest

SNUFF SAID

The taking of snuff, which was finely ground tobacco, became fashionable around 1680 at the height of buccaneer activity on the Spanish Main. Ships' wealthy passengers often carried elaborately decorated snuff boxes which made attractive trinkets for plunderers.

Garnet

Dutch snuff box made of copper alloy

Opal

Piracy and slavery

WHEN PIRATES CAPTURED a merchant ship, they often found a cargo of human misery. In the dark hold were hundreds of African slaves bound for the American colonies. The slave trade was big business in the 17th and 18th centuries, with slaves sold in the Americas for 10 to 15 times their cost in Africa. These huge profits lured the pirates. Some became slavers and others sold cargoes of slaves captured at sea. Many slipped easily between the occupations of slaver, privateer, and pirate – by the 1830s the term "picaroon" had come to mean both "pirate" and "slaver". But the end of the slave trade was in sight. Britain abolished slavery in 1833, and the newly founded United States of America followed some 30 years later.

CRUEL YOKE
This barbarous iron collar was designed to stop a slave from escaping through the bush. Savage punishments for re-captured runaways discouraged slaves from returning.

Heavy chain

DISHONOURABLE CAREER
John Hawkins (1532–95) was the first English privateer to realize that the slave trade was big business. In 1562 he made the first of three voyages as a slaver, sailing from England to West Africa, where he loaded 300 slaves. Hawkins then sailed to the Caribbean and sold his human cargo on the island of Hispaniola.

BUYING SLAVES
European slave traders bought slaves from African chiefs with cheap goods or bars of iron, brass, and copper, called manillas, which were used as money in West Africa.

Manillas

THE SLAVE TRADE TRIANGLE
Slave ships sailed from England or America with cargoes of cheap goods. In Africa, these were exchanged for slaves, and the ships sailed on to the Caribbean – this leg of the voyage was called the "middle passage". On islands like Jamaica, the slaves were exchanged for sugar, molasses, or hardwoods before the ships sailed home. A profit was made at every stage.

Britain, America, Caribbean, Atlantic, Jamaica, Africa, The middle passage

SLAVE REVOLT
Outnumbered by their cargo of slaves, the crew of a slave ship lived in constant fear of a revolt. Any rebellions were savagely repressed, but there was little chance of escaping from a slave ship. The odds for runaway slaves were greater if they managed to escape from a plantation.

Diagram showing the cramped, inhumane conditions inside a slave ship hold

DEATH SHIP
Many slaves died during the middle passage, so slavers packed as many slaves as possible into the holds. There was no sanitation and disease spread rapidly – the dead often lay alongside the living for days.

Long bar sticks out from the neck

Hook designed to catch on undergrowth to prevent a fast escape through the bush

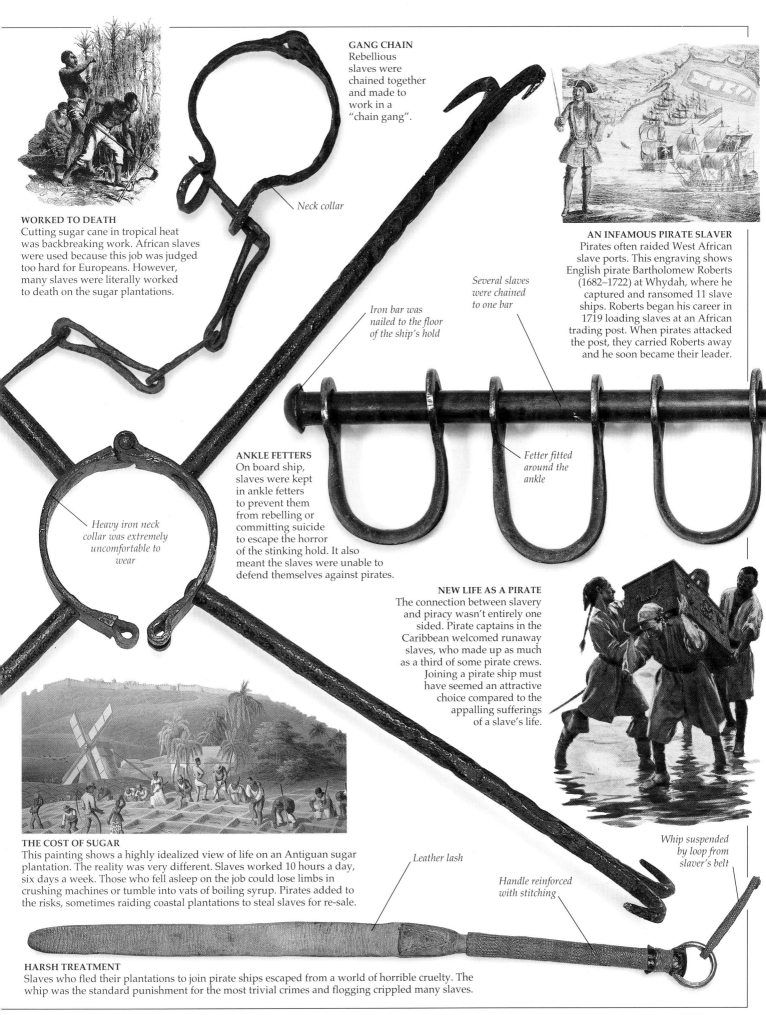

GANG CHAIN
Rebellious slaves were chained together and made to work in a "chain gang".

Neck collar

WORKED TO DEATH
Cutting sugar cane in tropical heat was backbreaking work. African slaves were used because this job was judged too hard for Europeans. However, many slaves were literally worked to death on the sugar plantations.

Iron bar was nailed to the floor of the ship's hold

Several slaves were chained to one bar

AN INFAMOUS PIRATE SLAVER
Pirates often raided West African slave ports. This engraving shows English pirate Bartholomew Roberts (1682–1722) at Whydah, where he captured and ransomed 11 slave ships. Roberts began his career in 1719 loading slaves at an African trading post. When pirates attacked the post, they carried Roberts away and he soon became their leader.

Heavy iron neck collar was extremely uncomfortable to wear

ANKLE FETTERS
On board ship, slaves were kept in ankle fetters to prevent them from rebelling or committing suicide to escape the horror of the stinking hold. It also meant the slaves were unable to defend themselves against pirates.

Fetter fitted around the ankle

NEW LIFE AS A PIRATE
The connection between slavery and piracy wasn't entirely one sided. Pirate captains in the Caribbean welcomed runaway slaves, who made up as much as a third of some pirate crews. Joining a pirate ship must have seemed an attractive choice compared to the appalling sufferings of a slave's life.

THE COST OF SUGAR
This painting shows a highly idealized view of life on an Antiguan sugar plantation. The reality was very different. Slaves worked 10 hours a day, six days a week. Those who fell asleep on the job could lose limbs in crushing machines or tumble into vats of boiling syrup. Pirates added to the risks, sometimes raiding coastal plantations to steal slaves for re-sale.

Leather lash

Handle reinforced with stitching

Whip suspended by loop from slaver's belt

HARSH TREATMENT
Slaves who fled their plantations to join pirate ships escaped from a world of horrible cruelty. The whip was the standard punishment for the most trivial crimes and flogging crippled many slaves.

Life at sea

LIFE ON A PIRATE SHIP was full of contrast. Seizing a prize meant moments of great excitement and terrifying danger. But in between there might be weeks of mind-numbing tedium. No wonder pirate crews quarrelled! If the "captain" was to control his crew's boredom and frustration he had to command respect – or fear – for many pirates ran their ships as democratic communities. If they couldn't agree on a course, they took a vote. Even the captain's job wasn't secure. If the crew disagreed with him, they held an election – this is how Bartholomew Sharp (p. 24) came to command a pirate cruise in 1680.

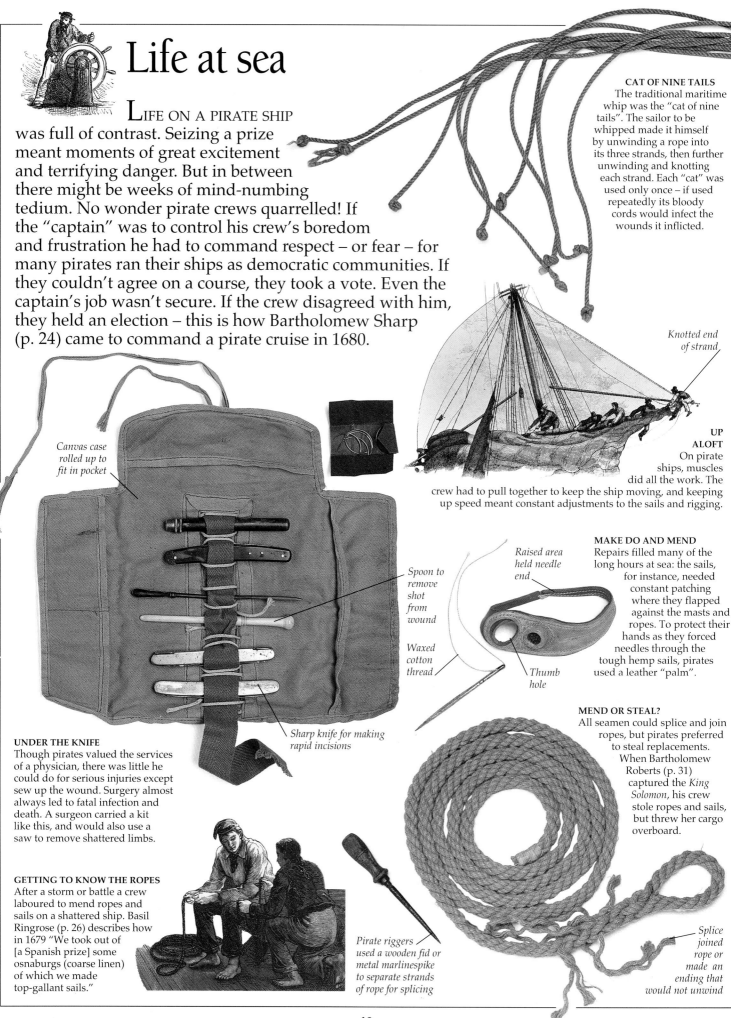

CAT OF NINE TAILS
The traditional maritime whip was the "cat of nine tails". The sailor to be whipped made it himself by unwinding a rope into its three strands, then further unwinding and knotting each strand. Each "cat" was used only once – if used repeatedly its bloody cords would infect the wounds it inflicted.

Knotted end of strand

UP ALOFT
On pirate ships, muscles did all the work. The crew had to pull together to keep the ship moving, and keeping up speed meant constant adjustments to the sails and rigging.

Canvas case rolled up to fit in pocket

Spoon to remove shot from wound

Raised area held needle end

Waxed cotton thread

Thumb hole

MAKE DO AND MEND
Repairs filled many of the long hours at sea: the sails, for instance, needed constant patching where they flapped against the masts and ropes. To protect their hands as they forced needles through the tough hemp sails, pirates used a leather "palm".

Sharp knife for making rapid incisions

UNDER THE KNIFE
Though pirates valued the services of a physician, there was little he could do for serious injuries except sew up the wound. Surgery almost always led to fatal infection and death. A surgeon carried a kit like this, and would also use a saw to remove shattered limbs.

MEND OR STEAL?
All seamen could splice and join ropes, but pirates preferred to steal replacements. When Bartholomew Roberts (p. 31) captured the *King Solomon*, his crew stole ropes and sails, but threw her cargo overboard.

GETTING TO KNOW THE ROPES
After a storm or battle a crew laboured to mend ropes and sails on a shattered ship. Basil Ringrose (p. 26) describes how in 1679 "We took out of [a Spanish prize] some osnaburgs (coarse linen) of which we made top-gallant sails."

Pirate riggers used a wooden fid or metal marlinespike to separate strands of rope for splicing

Splice joined rope or made an ending that would not unwind

Pirate contract

Some pirate crews had a code of conduct, which all agreed to obey. These rules, from Charles Johnson's 18th-century book on pirates, are typical:

I Every man has a vote in affairs of the moment; has equal title to the fresh provisions or strong liquors.

II No person to game at cards or dice for money.

III The lights and candles to be put out at eight o'clock at night.

IV To keep their piece [musket], pistols, and cutlass clean and fit for service.

V No boy or woman to be allowed amongst them.

VI To desert the ship in battle was punished with death or marooning.

Clean cords suggest that this "cat" was never used

Fabric covers rope to make handle

A FLOGGING
When they captured a vessel, pirates treated the officers much as they had in turn treated their crew. Captains who had imposed severe discipline, with floggings for minor offences, might get a taste of their own medicine on the pirate ship.

Yard arm

Swivel guns were quick to aim and load, but had short range

British flag (Red Ensign) was one of many the ship carried

Captain and a few other "officers" had cabins at stern

Barrels of drinking water (or rocks and gravel) helped balance ship

Space below deck was cramped, because ships carried enough pirates to crew prizes

PIRATE FLAGSHIP
Pirate ships varied widely. Small, fast sloops were ideal for inshore raiding, but much bigger vessels, such as this three-masted square-rigger, were safer on the open ocean. The size of the ship alone was enough to scare the wits out of many of the pirates' intended victims. This drawing is based on the only known wreck of a pirate ship, the *Whydah*, which sank off the coast of Wellfleet, Massachusetts in 1717.

FURRY FIEND
Every pirate ship had a population of rats. They were more than just a nuisance, for they devoured food, and could even gnaw their way right through the hull, sinking the vessel.

Food on board

"NOT BOILED TURTLE AGAIN?!" For hungry pirates the menu was short – when there was fresh meat, it was usually turtle. When turtles couldn't be found and the fish didn't bite, the pirates survived on biscuits or dried meat washed down with beer or wine. Monotony, however, was better than the starvation that pirates faced when shipwrecked or becalmed. Then they might be reduced to eating their satchels, or even each other. When food ran out on Charlotte de Berry's (p. 33) ship, the crew reputedly ate two black slaves, and then devoured her husband!

TASTY TUNA
In the Caribbean, pirates could catch fish fairly easily. Basil Ringrose recorded in his buccaneering journal that : "The sea hereabouts is very full of several sorts of fish, as dolphins, bonitos, albicores, mullets and old wives, etc. which came swimming about our ship in whole shoals."

A CLUBBED SANDWICH
Pirates lived off the land wherever they could. On remote islands, animals and birds were unused to being hunted and were often quite tame. The pirates could catch them with their bare hands.

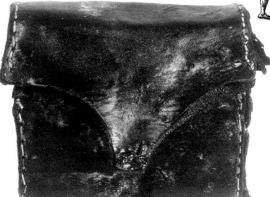

16th-century mariners clubbing tame turtle doves

PROVISIONING A SHIP
Even far from a port, a carefully chosen island could supply pirates with all the provisions they needed. These buccaneers are re-stocking their ship with fresh meat, water, and timber. In his journal of buccaneer life (p. 26), Ringrose recounts: "Having made this island, we resolved to go thither and refit our rigging and get some goats which there run wild."

POACHED POUCH
In 1670 Henry Morgan's (p. 27) band of half-starved buccaneers were so hungry that they resorted to eating their satchels! One of them left the recipe: "Slice the leather into pieces, then soak and beat and rub between stones to tenderise. Scrape off the hair, and roast or grill. Cut into smaller pieces and serve with lots of water."

Heavy shell makes the turtle slow on land

TURTLE HUNTERS
Captain Johnson (p. 61) recounts that: "The manner of catching [turtles] is very particular...As soon as they land, the men...turn them on their backs...and leave them until morning, where they are sure to find them, for they can't turn again, nor move from that place."

Large flippers for swimming

PIRATE PREY
Turtles were plentiful throughout the Caribbean and provided one of the few sources of fresh meat available to pirates. Agile in the sea, turtles were slow on land and easy prey for foraging pirates. On board ship, the cook could keep turtles alive in the hold until it was time to cook them. Soft-shelled turtle eggs were also a popular pirate delicacy.

FRESH EGGS
Like other ships of the 17th and 18th centuries, pirate vessels would have carried hens to provide fresh eggs and meat. The nautical nickname for eggs was "cackle-fruit", after the distinctive noise a hen makes when laying.

Hen's egg, a good source of protein

Hard-baked biscuit made of flour and water

HARD TACK
Long-lasting ship's biscuits were staple food for most mariners. They were known as "hard tack" because they were so tough. On board ship, biscuits soon became infested with weevils, so pirates preferred to eat them in the dark!

PREVENTATIVE MEDICINE
On long voyages, poor diet meant that pirates suffered from diseases such as scurvy, which is caused by a lack of vitamin C. However, in 1753 it was discovered that eating fresh fruit, particularly limes, could prevent scurvy.

Bottle for wine or brandy – favourite pirate drinks

SERVED ON A PLATE
Pirates ate from pewter plates like this one, but they were not well known for their table manners. Describing ravenous buccaneers, Exquemeling (p. 62) wrote: "Such was their hunger that they more resembled cannibals than Europeans..., the blood many times running down from their beards."

Plate made of pewter, an alloy of tin and lead

Expensive knife would have been pillaged from another ship

Fork folds into its handle, making it easy to carry in a pocket or pouch

KNIFE AND FORK ETIQUETTE
Although forks were sometimes used, rough pirates probably ate only with knives and spoons, or with their fingers.

A BOTTLE OF BEER
Without any method of preservation, water on board ship quickly became undrinkable, and all mariners preferred beer. Even naval vessels carried huge quantities of it, though usually in barrels rather than bottles.

Short of an opener, pirates just struck off the bottle neck with a cutlass

Earthenware beer bottle, 17th century

COOKING IN CALM SEAS
Captain Kidd's (p. 46) ship, *The Adventure Galley*, below, had no kitchen quarters, only a cauldron that was too dangerous to use in rough weather.

A JUG OF GROG
Washed down with half a gallon of plundered wine from a pewter tankard, almost any food became just about tolerable.

Life on land

CRAMMED TOGETHER FOR MONTHS on end in a stinking, often unseaworthy ship, pirates and buccaneers had plenty of time to dream about life on land. When they reached a port, many were wealthy enough to buy practically anything they'd dreamed of. They squandered their booty on drinking, women, and gambling, as one eyewitness recalled: "Such of these pirates are found who will spend two or three thousand pieces-of-eight in one night, not leaving themselves a good shirt of their backs". Two pieces-of-eight bought a cow, so the pirates gambled away the equivalent of a whole farm. Life on land wasn't always one long party, though. In between wild drinking bouts and gambling sessions, there was always work to be done. The crew had to careen and repair their ship, and take on board fresh water and provisions for the next villainous voyage.

MONEY CAN BUY YOU LOVE
Women were banned from most pirate ships, but they often came on board when the ships were moored in harbour. After a long voyage pirates usually went in search of female company. There were many women in Caribbean ports who were glad to share in the pirates' booty and join in their wild carousing.

Heavy handle swung with both hands

Mallet for striking the irons

Ramming iron

Caulking mallet

Jerry iron

Caulking iron

Pitch ladle

Pirates rest and careen their ship

Broad blade for splitting open rotten seams

Narrow blade for driving in new oakum

Angled blade for hacking old oakum from seams

CLEANED AND CAREENED
Seaweed and barnacles grew rapidly on the bottom of ships, greatly reducing their speed. Worse, worms bored tiny holes that could eventually sink the ship. Pirate crews solved the problem by regular careening, which meant beaching the ship to repair the hull.

Adze

Strong, chisel-like blade for careening – chipping off barnacles and weed

TOOLS OF THE TRADE
Wooden ships required regular maintenance if they were to remain seaworthy. Pirate crews had tools like these to carry out essential jobs. Caulking, which involved repairing the seams between planks, was vital to keep the ship watertight. The seams were stripped, filled with unravelled rope, or oakum, and sealed with hot pitch.

Funnel-like tip for pouring hot pitch into seams

Silver rim

BLACK JACK
Dockside taverns welcomed thirsty pirates. There the pirates washed the salt from their throats with copious quantities of beer and wine, probably drinking from "black jacks" – leather tankards made watertight and rigid with a coating of pitch.

MIDNIGHT REVELLING
In this picture, the crews of Blackbeard (pp. 30–31) and Charles Vane are carousing the night away on Ocracoke Island off the North Carolina coast. Not all ports welcomed pirates, and crews often holed up in a favourite pirate hideaway to celebrate a successful raid.

17th century playing cards commemorating a famous political plot

A HAND OF CARDS
Gambling for money was forbidden on board many pirate ships, probably because it caused fights. On shore, the pirate crews could soon be parted from their share of a prize by a crooked card game.

Wooden dice

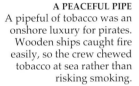

SPENDING SPREES
Pirates were welcome in many ports, since crews were famous for spending money with wild abandon on "things of little value".

BUCCANEER BASE
Port Royal in Jamaica, above, was a magnet for 17th-century pirates seeking pleasure ashore. British governors welcomed the pirates' custom, believing their presence would protect the island from Spanish attacks. In 1692 Port Royal was destroyed by an earthquake which many believed was divine judgement on this corrupt town.

A PEACEFUL PIPE
A pipeful of tobacco was an onshore luxury for pirates. Wooden ships caught fire easily, so the crew chewed tobacco at sea rather than risking smoking.

Clay pipe stem has snapped off

Lid to keep out flies

YO HO HO AND A BOTTLE OF RUM
Pirates' reputation as rum-swilling bandits was largely true. They drank anything alcoholic, and many were never sober while onshore. One notorious drunk would buy a huge barrel of wine, and "placing it in the street, would force everyone who passed by to drink with him; threatening also to pistol them, in case they would not do it".

TANKARD UP
Glass was costly and fragile, so the keepers of most taverns greeted pirates with brimming pewter tankards. These were strong enough to withstand a night of revelry.

17th-century liquor bottles

OLD CALABAR CAREENAGE
A secluded beach was essential for careening because pirates were defenceless during the work. Old Calabar River on the Guinea coast of Africa was an ideal spot because it was too shallow for men-of-war to pursue the pirates' small craft. In the picture above, Bartholomew Robert's (p. 39) crew relax by the river after a hard day's caulking.

Pirates of the Indian Ocean

Kidd buries his bible in a mythical episode from his life

WHEN THE RICH PICKINGS on the Spanish Main (p. 20) declined, many pirates sailed east to the Indian Ocean. They were lured by the treasure fleets of the Indian Moghul and the great merchantmen of the British, French, and Dutch East India Companies. Most of the pirates made for Madagascar off the east coast of Africa. This wild island was ideally placed for raiding European trade routes to India and Muslim pilgrimage routes to the Red Sea. The pirates soon amassed large fortunes and the likes of Kidd and Avery acquired legendary status. But their activities damaged trade and aroused anti-European feeling in India, causing governments to act against the pirates.

An East Indiaman

CAPTAIN KIDD
Scottish-born William Kidd (c.1645–1701) was a New York businessman sent to the Indian Ocean to hunt Avery and his colleagues. However, under pressure from his ruffianly crew, Kidd committed several acts of piracy himself. On his return, Kidd was tried and hanged as a pirate.

Avery captured the Gang-i-Sawai *near the River Indus*

Mecca

Red Sea

India   China

Surat

Africa

Sumatra

Indian Ocean

Java

Madagascar

Cape of Good Hope

GOOD HOPE FOR PIRATES
After rounding the Cape of Good Hope, European trade ships took one of two different courses on their way to India and China. But both routes passed within a few hundred miles of Madagascar, the pirates' island lair.

Ratlines hanging from the rigging enabled sailors to climb above the deck; once aloft, they were better able to fight off an attack from a pirate ship

GLITTERING PRIZES
Indian ships seized by pirates yielded rich hauls of gems. One of Avery's crew who raided the *Gang-i-Sawai* recalled: "We took great quantities of jewels and a saddle and bridle set with rubies."

EAST INDIAMAN
Laden with luxury goods, East Indiamen were the favourite prey of pirates. These great merchant ships traded between Europe and Asia in the 17th and 18th centuries. On the journey to Asia, the East Indiamen were loaded with gold and silver; they carried fine china, silks, and spices back to Europe from the East.

PRICELESS PORCELAIN
Fine Chinese porcelain was highly prized in 17th- and 18th-century Europe. After 1684, when the Chinese allowed the British East India Company to open a trading station at Canton, the East Indiamen carried tons of "china" across the Indian Ocean.

PIRATE PARADISE
The tropical island paradise of Madagascar acquired an exotic reputation. Popular legends told how the pirates there lived like princes. According to Captain Johnson (p. 61): "They married the most beautiful of the negro women, not one or two but as many as they liked."

A BRILLIANT CAREER
The English pirate Henry Avery (1665–c.1728) became notorious for his capture of the Indian Moghul's ship *Gang-i-Sawai*, which was carrying pilgrims and treasure from Surat to Mecca. The brutal treatment of the passengers aroused a furious response from the Moghul who demanded retribution from the British authorities.

During battles sailors stood on the maintop to fire at the pirate ships

St Mary's Island

HIGH SOCIETY PIRATE
American-born Thomas Tew led what became known as "the pirate round", sailing from North America to the Indian Ocean and returning with booty. At home he was a celebrity and is seen here relating his adventures to his friend the governor of New York. Tew was killed on an expedition with Avery in 1695.

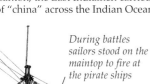

SAFE HAVEN
More like a small continent than an island, Madagascar was an ideal hideout for the pirates of the Indian Ocean. In the late 17th century this wild, tropical island was uncolonized by Europeans and therefore safe for outlaws. All the same, the ever-wary pirates created a fortified base at St Mary's Island on Madagascar's north-east coast which could be easily defended if necessary.

East Indiaman is heavily armed to resist attack by pirates

Tea leaves

Pepper

Green coffee beans

Cloves

SURPLUS SPICE
Pirates who captured a cargo of spices from an East Indiaman often dumped their haul, because spices were bulky and difficult to sell. In 1720 a Madagascar beach was reported to be a foot deep in pepper and cloves.

Large hold for carrying bulky cargoes and provisions for many weeks made the ship slow and cumbersome

Nutmegs

Cinnamon sticks

COSTLY CUPPA
Cargoes of tea and coffee could fetch a big profit in Europe (in 1700 a pound of tea cost more than two weeks' wages for a labourer) but pirates preferred to capture wine or brandy! Only one pirate, Bartholomew Roberts (p. 39), preferred tea to alcohol; he thought drunkeness impaired a ship's efficiency.

Desert islands

M<small>AROONED ALONE ON AN ISLAND</small>, a disgraced pirate watched helplessly as his ship sailed away. A desert island was a prison without walls. The sea prevented escape and the chances of being rescued were slim. Although marooned pirates were left with a few essential provisions, starvation faced those who could not hunt and fish. This cruel punishment was meted out to pirates who stole from their comrades or deserted their ship in battle. When leaky pirate ships ran aground, survivors of the wreck faced the same lonely fate.

THE CASTAWAY
Shipwrecked pirates endured the same sense of isolation as those marooned for a crime. Their only hope of rescue was to watch for a sail on the horizon.

BARE NECESSITIES
A marooned pirate was put ashore with only meagre supplies. English captain John Phillips' pirate code stated that the victim should be provided with: "one bottle of Powder, one bottle of water, one small arm, and shot". But the unlucky man had no way of cooking or keeping warm. One kind pirate secretly gave a marooned man: "a tinder box with materials in it for striking fire; which, in his circumstances, was a greater present than gold or jewels."

DEFENCE
A pistol was useful for defence against wild beasts, but a musket was better for hunting.

A DAY'S GRACE
A small bottle of water lasted just a day or so. After that the castaway had to find his own.

ALEXANDER SELKIRK
Sick of arguments on his ship, Scottish privateer Alexander Selkirk (1676–1721) actually asked to be marooned. By the time he'd changed his mind, the ship had sailed away. To amuse himself, the castaway tamed wild cats and goats and taught them to dance.

THE FORGOTTEN ISLE
Alexander Selkirk's home from 1704 to 1709 was a small island in the South Pacific 640 kms (400 miles) west of Chile. One of the Juan Fernandez islands, Más á Tierra had an abundant supply of water and teemed with wild pigs and goats. Selkirk lived largely on goat meat and palm cabbage and dressed in goatskins. When he was found by his rescuers, he was ragged and dirty, but was unenthusiastic about leaving his island home.

ROBINSON CRUSOE

This most famous of all fictional castaways was the creation of English author Daniel Defoe (1660–1731). He based the story on the life of Alexander Selkirk, but gave Crusoe a "savage" companion, Man Friday. Crusoe spent more than a quarter of a century on his island, and lived more comfortably than any real castaway: "in this plentiful manner, I lived; neither could I be said to want anything but society".

A LONELY FATE

In this imaginative painting by Howard Pyle, a lonely pirate awaits death on the beach of a desert island. In fact, marooned pirates didn't have time to brood on their fate. Most who survived stress how busy they were foraging for food and water or building shelters.

Gunpowder

Musket balls

Powder horn

SHIPWRECKED

Pirates often took over a captured vessel, but if the ship was unseaworthy, they could easily find themselves shipwrecked on a deserted shore. The same fate befell pirate crews who became drunk, which was fairly common, and neglected navigation.

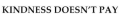

KINDNESS DOESN'T PAY

English pirate Edward England (died 1720) fell out with his crew while sailing off the coast of Africa. Accused of being too kind to a prisoner, England and two others were marooned by their merciless comrades on the island of Mauritius. According to one account, the three escaped by building a boat and sailing to Madagascar, where England died soon after.

IN SHORT SUPPLY

The gunpowder stored in this powder horn would soon run out, and after that castaways had to be ingenious. One group of pirates marooned in the Bahamas lived by "feeding upon berries and shell fish [and] sometimes catching a stingray… by the help of a sharpened stick".

The French corsairs

THE FRENCH KNEW ST MALO as "La Cité Corsaire", but to the English, it was a "nest of wasps". By any name, the French port of St Malo in the 17th century was a town grown rich on the profits of privateering. For many local people privateering, or "la course", was a family trade, one in which son followed father to sea. The French corsairs emerged in the 9th century when the merchant ships of Brittany armed themselves against the marauding Vikings. When the Viking threat ended during the 11th century there was no shortage of targets, for France was frequently at war. England was most often the victim of the wasps' sting, and in 1693 the English built an "infernal machine" to destroy the nest. However, their floating bomb exploded noisily in St Malo harbour with just one French casualty – a cat. The English fleet sailed away humiliated, and the corsairs continued well into the next century.

RÉNÉ DUGUAY-TROUIN
The most well-known of the French corsairs, Duguay-Trouin (1673–1736) was in command of a 40-gun ship by the age of 21. In a career that spanned 23 years he captured 16 battleships and 300 merchant vessels.

PISTOLS OF A PRIVATEER
Robert Surcouf was famous not only for his brilliance as a corsair, but also for his personal bravery. His handsome pistols were not just decoration – Surcouf once took on a dozen Prussian soldiers in a fight and won.

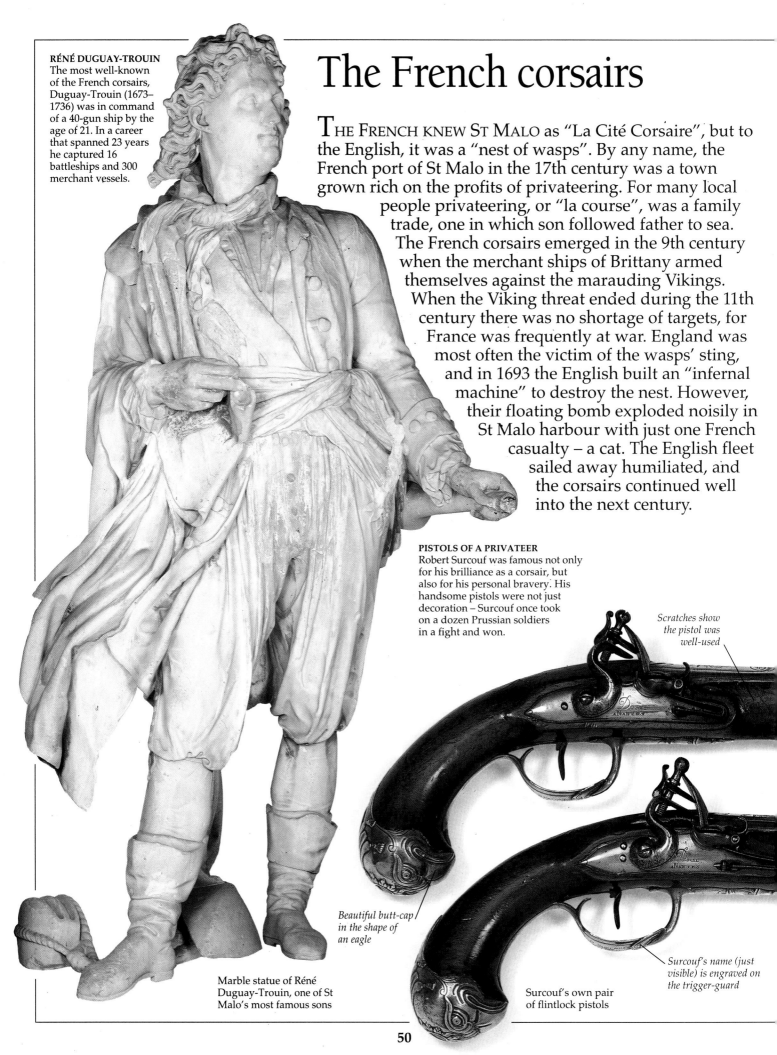

Scratches show the pistol was well-used

Beautiful butt-cap in the shape of an eagle

Marble statue of Réné Duguay-Trouin, one of St Malo's most famous sons

Surcouf's name (just visible) is engraved on the trigger-guard

Surcouf's own pair of flintlock pistols

HEROES OF THE HIGH SEAS

Renowned for their daring deeds, the French corsairs were national heroes. They were famous because they were patriots fighting for France, but also because privateering was profitable. Many Brittany families grew rich on the proceeds, and even the Bishop of St Malo invested in "la course". Ships and streets were named after the corsairs: this romantic ship's figurehead portrays Duguay-Trouin.

17th-century ship's figurehead

Brass barrel

Ramrod

DUNKIRK
Home town of Jean Bart, Dunkirk was hot property while he was a boy: it was by turn Spanish, French, and English territory. Finally in French hands, the port became a corsair base to rival St Malo.

DVNKIRK.

JEAN BART
Jean Bart (1651–1702) preyed on ships in the English Channel and North Sea. Famed for his daring, he escaped to France by rowing 150 miles in a small boat when captured by the hated English.

ROBERT SURCOUF
Born a century after Duguay-Trouin, Robert Surcouf (1773–1827), left, practised the corsair trade far from his St Malo home. His base was the French-owned island of Mauritius in the Indian Ocean. From there he raided British merchant ships heading for Indian ports.

CAPTURING THE *KENT*
Surcouf's most heroic feat was to capture the British East Indiaman *Kent*. This painting shows Surcouf's men boarding the huge 38-gun merchantman from their much smaller ship, the *Confiance*. One of the captured crew sneered that the French fought only for profit, whereas the English fought for honour, to which Surcouf wittily replied: "That only proves that each of us fights to acquire something he does not possess."

Missiles

Incendiary bombs

Barrels of explosives

AN INFERNAL DISASTER
This infernal machine, right, was sent against the Malouins by the English as a lethal weapon. Packed full of explosives, this 26 m (85 ft) long bomb ship sat high in the water so that it could sail close to St Malo's city wall. But on the night of the attack, the ship hit a rock, sea-water damped the gunpowder, and the bomb went off like a damp squib.

Barrels of gunpowder

THE CORSAIR CAPITAL
The corsair promoters, or "armateurs", of St Malo flourished. By the 18th century, when this view was drawn, they had become so wealthy that even the French king Louis XIV (1643–1715) borrowed money from them to pay for his wars.

American privateers

THE AMERICAN REVOLUTION (1775–83) showed off the power of the privateers as few wars had done before. The tiny Continental (American) Navy fought their English rulers with just 34 ships. But 13 times this number of privateers attacked British *merchant* shipping, crippling trade. One 18th-century English writer complained: "...all commerce with America is at an end...survey our docks; count there the gallant ships laid up and useless". As in previous wars, those who lost ships to privateers dismissed them as "pirates". English victims used the term loosely, even applying it to Continental Navy officers, such as John Paul Jones. After independence, when war with Britain broke out again in 1812, the newly founded United States of America used privateers to boost its naval strength once more. But the speedy ships were never again as effective as in the days when they helped to secure their nation's freedom.

DASHING NAVAL HERO
Daring raids on the coastal lands of Britain earned John Paul Jones the label of "pirate" in the country of his birth, but it was his actions at sea that made him well known in the USA. In his most famous battle, he manoeuvred his vessel alongside a British warship and lashed the two together. British guns almost sank his ship, but Jones dismissed calls to surrender with the words: "I have not yet begun to fight!" Three hours later, the British gave in.

AFRICAN PRIZES
An Englishman writing from Grenada in 1777 complained bitterly that the American privateers had captured "some thousand weight of gold dust".

HUMBLE CARGOES
Ships captured by privateers did not always contain costly luxuries. Ordinary foods such as salt and rice fed revolutionary American troops – and their loss starved the British foe.

Rice

ELEPHANT TEETH
American-bound experts lost to privateers in the Revolutionary War included a cargo of ivory. Insurance costs rose six-fold for ships sailing without protection.

Salt

UNARMED COMBAT
The largest colonial port, Philadelphia equipped many plucky privateers. One of them, the brig *Despatch*, sailed unarmed from this port in 1776, hoping to capture guns from a British ship in the Atlantic! Amazingly, the crew succeeded within a few days, and sailed on to France.

PATRIOT'S BUST
Neither pirate nor privateer, Scots-born John Paul Jones (1747–92) was in some ways a bit of both. Apprenticed to the sea on a slaver, he fled the Caribbean to escape a murder charge. His career in the Continental Navy began in 1775, and Jones' daring deeds over the next six years made him an American national hero. He won promotion, but political rivalry later in life left him bitter and broken, and he died in 1792.

BLUFFING PRIVATEER
Jonathan Haraden (1745–1803) once sailed alongside an English ship, hoisted the bloody flag, and demanded surrender in five minutes. Then he stood watch with a lighted taper by a cannon and waited. The ship surrendered, but Haraden was bluffing – the cannon was loaded with his only remaining shot.

TOPSAIL SCHOONER
American privateers who used specially built ships favoured topsail schooners like the vessel shown here outside New Orleans harbour. These very fast, fairly small ships had two masts, the foremast shorter than the main mast. Rigging a square sail at the top of the foremast boosted speed with a following wind.

PRIVATEER CITY
With a natural harbour in Chesapeake Bay, Baltimore was a traditional shipbuilding centre. Some of the first privateering vessels of the Revolutionary War sailed from this Maryland city – at first converted merchant ships, but later purpose-built schooners.

JEAN LAFITTE
Haiti-born pirate, privateer, slaver, and smuggler, Jean Lafitte (c.1780–c.1826) and his brother Pierre ran an underworld gang that provided about one-tenth of the jobs in New Orleans around 1807. Outlawed for smuggling slaves, Lafitte earned a pardon by defending the city against attack in the war of 1812.

GULF ATTACK
The Lafittes' pirate attacks were mainly on Spanish vessels in the Gulf of Mexico. They claimed that these raids were legitimate privateering, and held letters of marque (p. 18) to prove it. But they also took American prizes, and secretly traded in slaves through their stronghold at Barataria Bay near New Orleans.

Pirates of the China seas

FORMIDABLE JUNK
The largest Chinese pirate junks were converted cargo vessels armed with 10-15 guns. They were formidable fighting ships and the Chinese navy was unable to crush them, as Admiral Tsuen Mow Sun complained in 1809: "The pirates are too powerful, we cannot master them by our arms…".

Three masts with four-sided sails of bamboo matting

Captain and his family had quarters at the stern of the ship. Crew lived in the cramped hold

THE SEAS AND CHANNELS OF CHINA and Southeast Asia were a pirate's paradise. Small boats could hide easily in the mangrove swamps along the coasts. Pirates were exploiting this by AD 400, combining sea-robbery with local warfare. China and Japan often had to act together to suppress them. When Europeans set up empires in the 16th and 17th centuries, the situation worsened. Pirates such as Ching Yih had over 500 ships. Ching-Chi-ling commanded a fleet of 1,000 heavily armed vessels in the 17th century, together with many slaves and bodyguards. The Europeans acted against these powerful pirates and by the 1860s had stamped them out.

BARBER PIRATE
Hong Kong barber Chui Apoo joined the fleet of pirate chief Shap'n'gtzai in 1845 and was soon appointed his lieutenant.

THE END OF THE ROAD
British navy gunboats destroyed Chui Apoo's fleet in 1849 as part of a campaign against pirate chief Shap'n'gtzai.

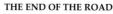

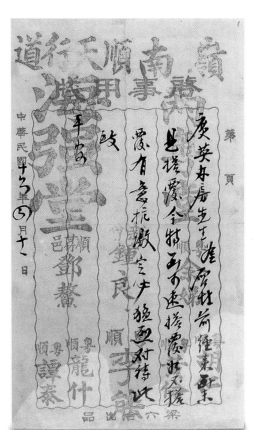

PAY UP OR ELSE
19th-century Chinese pirates used to extort money from coastal villages. They threatened to destroy the town and enslave the occupants if the ransom was not paid. In this later ransom note pirates demand money in return for not attacking shipping.

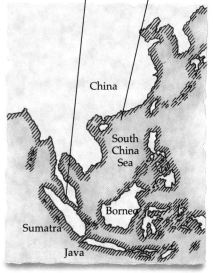

Strait of Malacca was a hunting ground for pirates

Mouth of Canton River was pirate centre from the 1760s

China

South China Sea

Borneo

Sumatra

Java

THE SEAS OF SOUTHEAST ASIA
Though large fleets sometimes dominated piracy in eastern Asia, smaller tribal groups cruised over limited areas.

PIRATE PENNANT

The fleets of the China Sea pirates were divided into squadrons, each with its own flag: Ching Yih's fleet had red, yellow, green, blue, black, and white flag groups, and flag carriers led the attack when the pirates boarded a ship. This elaborate flag shows the mythical empress of heaven T'ien Hou, calmer of storms and protector of merchant ships.

Though the pirates worshipped T'ien Hou, she was also sacred to those who opposed piracy

Bats were a good-luck symbol — their name in Chinese, "fu", is a pun on "good fortune"

LAST STAND

The British navy destroyed the most notorious Chinese pirate fleet in 1849. Anchored at the mouth of the Haiphong River in northern Vietnam, Shap'n'gtzai thought he was safe. But when the tide turned it swung the pirate junks round so that their guns pointed at each other. The British ships were able to pick them off one by one.

Naval surgeon Edward Cree captured the destruction of Shap'n'gtzai's fleet in a vivid watercolour painting in his journal

TWO-HANDED HACKER

For hand-to-hand fighting the traditional weapon of Chinese pirates was a long, heavy sword. Swung with both hands, the blade could even cut through metal armour. Japanese pirates preferred smaller swords: they fought with one in each hand and could defeat even the most skilled Chinese warrior.

Punishment

"DANCING THE HEMPEN JIG" was the punishment for pirates caught and convicted of their crimes. The "hempen jig" was the dance of death at the end of the hangman's hemp rope. Pirates joked about execution, but this bravado often vanished when they were faced with the gallows. However for most pirates the everyday dangers of life at sea were more of a hazard than the hangman. Relatively few were brought to justice, and even those found guilty were often pardoned. For privateers, capture meant only imprisonment, with the possibility of freedom in an exchange of prisoners. But many privateers feared prison; gaols were disease-ridden places from which many never returned.

Head of a pirate displayed on a pike

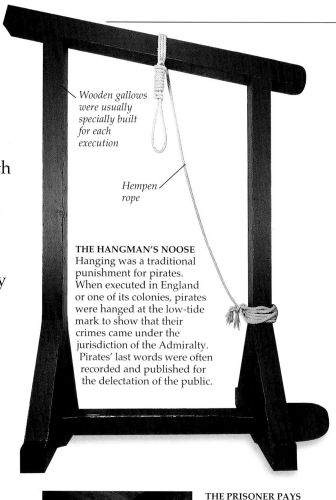

Wooden gallows were usually specially built for each execution

Hempen rope

THE HANGMAN'S NOOSE
Hanging was a traditional punishment for pirates. When executed in England or one of its colonies, pirates were hanged at the low-tide mark to show that their crimes came under the jurisdiction of the Admiralty. Pirates' last words were often recorded and published for the delectation of the public.

PRISON HULKS
Britain introduced these floating prisons in 1776. Moored in the estuary of the river Thames, hulks were first made from naval ships that were no longer seaworthy. Later hulks were specially built as floating gaols. Conditions inside a prison hulk were damp and unhealthy, and being consigned to one was the severest punishment apart from the death sentence.

THE PRISONER PAYS
A solitary cell such as this one would have been viewed as luxury accommodation by a captive pirate. Prison cells in the 17th and 18th centuries were crowded to bursting point, and only those who could afford to bribe the turnkey (gaoler) could hope to live in decent conditions. Prisoners paid for candles, food, and even for the right to get close to the feeble fire that warmed the dank dungeon.

THE PONTON
Captured French corsairs dreaded English prison hulks, which they called pontons. One wrote in 1797: "For the last eight days we have been reduced to eating dogs, cats and rats…the only rations we get consist of mouldy bread… rotten meat, and brackish water."

Extension to ship may have been the prison-ship's galley

Laundry hung out to dry

Prisoners lived in the damp, stinking hold

Ventilation through tiny windows was poor

Soldier guards the prison hulk

THE END OF THE LINE

Like many a pirate's hanging, that of Stede Bonnet in 1718 was a public event. The people of Charleston in the southern United States crowded the docks to get a view. The once dashing Major Bonnet had begged the Governor for a reprieve, but his pleas were in vain.

Skull of an 18th-century murderer

HANGING IN CHAINS

The bodies of executed pirates were often hung from a wooden frame called a gibbet to warn others not to repeat their crimes. The corpse was chained into an iron cage to prevent relatives from taking it down and burying it. A condemned man was measured for his gibbet chains before his execution and pirates were said to fear this even more than hanging.

Tight-fitting cage ensured the bones stayed in place once the flesh had rotted

Broad iron band enclosed the arms and chest

Gibbet cage was made to measure by a blacksmith

Handcuffs

NO ESCAPE

Pirates were often put in chains to prevent an attempt at escape. Before being shipped to England, the unfortunate William Kidd spent the winter of 1699 secured in Boston gaol by manacles weighing more than 7 kg (16 lb).

Early 19th-century ankle fetters

ABANDON HOPE ALL YE WHO ENTER

William Kidd and other pirates walked through this grim gate into London's infamous Newgate Prison. Kidd was held in this foul, overcrowded gaol for an entire year. By the time he came to trial, he was in no fit state to defend himself.

18th-century gibbet cage

A GRIM REMINDER

The hanging of William Kidd (p. 46) in 1701 drew a large crowd to London's Execution Dock. After the first rope snapped, Kidd was hanged at the second attempt. His corpse was chained to a post to be washed three times by the tide, according to Admiralty law. Kidd's body was then covered in tar to make it last and hung in chains at Tilbury Point where it served as a warning to all seamen sailing in or out of the River Thames.

The pirates defeated

AFTER FLOURISHING for 5,000 years, organized piracy and privateering finally ended in the 19th century. When the century began, privateers were still a dangerous nuisance – yet the navies of big maritime powers no longer needed the help of privately owned warships. So in 1856 most maritime nations signed a treaty, the Declaration of Paris, banning letters of marque (p. 18). New technology also helped to end piracy. The 19th century was the age of steam power, and the British and U.S. navies built steam ships that could sail almost anywhere, even on a windless day. Pirates, who still relied on sail, were easily trapped by the steamers. By 1850 only small pirate bands were left.

NEVER A FIGURE OF FUN
The British Navy took strong action against Malaysian and Indonesian pirates suspected of damaging trade. This colourful pantomime figurehead once decorated the bows of HMS *Harlequin*, a British navy sloop involved in anti-piracy action. In 1844, the *Harlequin* and two other ships sailed from Penang on a mission to punish pirates from Achin in north Sumatra. The captains of this little fleet could not identify the pirates they were seeking, so they indiscriminately burned down riverside houses.

HEAD OF A PIRATE
Blackbeard's head was suspended from the *Pearl*'s bowsprit (the spar at the front of the ship).

LAST-DITCH BATTLE
In 1718 Lieutenant Maynard of HMS *Pearl* was commissioned to capture Blackbeard (pp. 30–31) dead or alive. When he tracked down the arch pirate, Maynard engaged him in a legendary duel. According the Captain Johnson, Blackbeard: "fought with great fury until he received five-and-twenty wounds, and five of them by shot" before he died.

STEAMING IN ON THE PIRATES

The first steam ships had masts and sails, but they could also be propelled by paddle wheels. Pirates ignored the smoking vessels when they first saw them, assuming they were sailing ships on fire. Their nonchalance ended when the steamers sailed directly against the wind (impossible in a sailing ship) to capture them.

POLICE DOG

When HMS *Greyhound* sighted two ships to the east of Long Island, America, the crew had no idea what dangerous pirates they were tangling with. The ships belonged to the infamous Edward Low (p. 30) and his crew. After an eight-hour battle, the *Greyhound* was victorious. The pirates were brought to justice in the summer of 1723 when 26 of them were hanged.

THE SWALLOW

In the 18th century, the British Navy's ultimate "pirate buster" was the man-of-war, a huge sailing fortress that could out-gun the most powerful pirate ship. The man-of-war *Swallow* brought an end to the career of notorious pirate Bartholomew Roberts (p. 31) off the west African coast in 1722. Roberts foolishly sailed into a battle against the warship, and was shot in the neck.

BOMBING BARBARY

Corsairs sailing from the Barbary states (pp. 14–15) renewed their attacks during the Napoleonic Wars (1796–15). When peace returned, the United States and the European powers acted to crush the Barbary pirates for good. In 1816 British and Dutch ships bombarded Algiers, forcing the Bey to release prisoners and apologise for the pirates' actions. France occupied Algiers 14 years later.

CELEBRATING VICTORY

Inscribed "Algiers bombarded and its fleet destroyed and Christian slavery extinguished", this gold medal celebrates the successful British and Dutch bombardment of Algiers.

View of the Swallow's bows

Due to naval cutbacks, figurehead has less elaborate carving than on earlier ships

Imprisoned pirates from Roberts' ship were held in manacles in the hold

Roberts was killed by grapeshot from one of these guns

With 50 cannon and a highly trained crew, the Swallow easily outgunned Roberts' Royal Fortune and its ragged pirate band

Side view of the Swallow

Pirates in literature

ALMOST AS SOON as the world's navies had made the oceans safe, people began to forget the pirates' murderous ways. Many writers turned pirates from thieves into rascals or heroes. But books do not always paint a romantic picture of piracy. Some, such as *Buccaneers of America*, tell true pirate stories in blood-curdling detail. And in the most famous of all fictional tales, *Treasure Island*, the pirates are villains to be feared. Yet even this classic adventure yarn revolves around the search for a buried hoard of gold. Like walking the plank, buried treasure is exciting and colourful – but fiction nonetheless.

CAPTAIN FLINT
"Pieces of eight!" Long John Silver's parrot called out for the fictional pirate's favourite booty.

BYRONIC HERO
English poet Lord Byron (1788–1824) did much to create the myth of the romantic pirate. He wrote his famous poem *The Corsair* at a time when the pirate menace was only a few years in the past. Byron excuses the crimes of his hero with the rhyme: "He knew himself a villain but he deem'd The rest no better than the thing he seem'd."

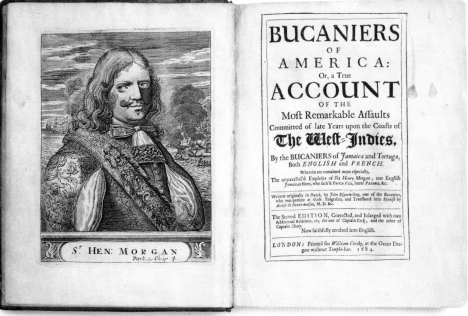

TRUE STORIES OF PIRATE VILLAINY
Alexander Exquemeling (1645–1707) provided one of the few eyewitness accounts of 17th-century piracy. A Frenchman, he sailed with buccaneers in the Caribbean. His descriptions of their cruelty, first published in Dutch in 1678, are still capable of making the reader feel physically sick.

PIRATE WITH PARROT
When Scots writer Robert Louis Stevenson (1850–94) created Long John Silver, he invented a pirate who has influenced writers ever since. Silver quickly gains the treasure-seekers' trust in *Treasure Island* (1883), only to betray them later.

IN SEARCH OF TREASURE
In *Treasure Island* Jim Hawkins, who tells the story, sets sail in the *Hispaniola* to unearth a pirate's buried booty. Jim overhears a plan by Silver and Israel Hands to capture the ship and kill the crew.

MYTHICAL MAP
The key to the treasure in Stevenson's book is an island map and cryptic clues. No real pirate left such convenient directions to a fortune.

WALKING TO A WATERY GRAVE

The Boston stationer Charles Ellms published *The Pirates' Own Book* in 1837. A mixture of myth and "true" pirate stories, it quickly became a best seller. Ellms described the pirate punishment of "walking the plank", but there is no clear evidence that any pirate drowned captives by forcing them off the end of a board suspended over the side of the ship.

IN A TIGHT CORNER

"One more step, Mr Hands … and I'll blow your brains out." Mutinous buccaneer Israel Hands ignored Jim Hawkins' warning, only to be sent plunging to his death by a blast from the boy's flintlock. Robert Louis Stevenson borrowed the name for this fictional villain from Blackbeard's real-life first mate.

MYSTERY HISTORY

A General History of the Robberies and Murders of the Most Notorious Pyrates was published in 1724. It describes the exploits of pirates such as Blackbeard, Bartholomew Roberts, Mary Read, and Anne Bonny within a few years of their capture or execution. The book inspired many later works of fiction, but the true identity of its author, Captain Charles Johnson, is a mystery.

Peter and Hook fought for their lives on a slippery rock, but only Peter fought fairly

PAN AND HOOK

Peter Pan's adversary Captain Hook was in fiction "Blackbeard's bosun", and author J.M. Barrie took some of Hook's character from the real pirate Edward Teach (pp. 30–31). "His hair was dressed in long curls which at a little distance looked like black candles."

Peter's gang of boys bravely fought the stronger pirates

PIRATES ON THE PAGE

Thousands of children saw Peter Pan on stage. But as the book *Peter and Wendy* it charmed millions more. Set on a magic island and a pirate ship, the story tells of the defeat of the pirates by a boy who never grew up.

Pirates in film and theatre

S WAGGERING ON THE SCREEN or swooping across the stage, a pirate provided dramatists with a ready-made yet adaptable character. He could play a black-hearted villain, a carefree adventurer, a romantic hero, or a blameless outlaw. Theatrical pirates first trod the boards in 1612, but it was *The Successful Pirate* a century later that really established the theme. Movie makers were also quick to exploit the swashbuckling glamour of the pirate life. Screen portrayals of piracy began in the era of the silent films and they remain a box-office draw to this day.

THESPIAN PIRATE
This 19th-century souvenir shows an actor called Pitt playing the pirate Will Watch, with the standard pirate props.

Puppet's head is made of wood

STAGE SUIT
Neatly pressed stage costumes contrast vividly with the rags that real pirates wore. Most real pirates changed their clothes only when they raided a ship and stole a new set.

Curved cutlass

PUPPET PARODY
The action and speed of buccaneering stories makes them a natural choice for puppet theatres. In a crude satire of pirate style, these two 19th-century glove puppets depict English and Spanish pirates. The simply dressed English pirate carries the short, curved cutlass; his dapper Spanish counterpart holds a rapier.

NEVERLAND COMES TO TINSELTOWN
In Steven Spielberg's remake of the Peter Pan story *Hook*, Dustin Hoffman played the title role.

English pirate puppet

CORSAIR CRAZY
In the early 1950s pirate movies were very popular – nine films appeared between 1950 and 1953. The *Crimson Pirate*, starring Burt Lancaster (1952) was one of the best.

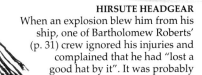

HIRSUTE HEADGEAR
When an explosion blew him from his ship, one of Bartholomew Roberts' (p. 31) crew ignored his injuries and complained that he had "lost a good hat by it". It was probably not as grand as this costume hat.

SWASHBUCKLER'S SCARF
Early pirate movies may have favoured red and yellow props such as this sash because they showed up better than other colours on the primitive Technicolor film system. Burning ships were popular for the same reason.

Spanish pirate puppet

SHOW DOWN
Hollywood told the true story of pirate Anne Bonny (p. 33) in *Anne of the Indies* (1951), but the temptation to dress up history was, as usual, too much to resist. The movie pitted Anne, played by American actress Jean Peters (born 1926) against her "former boss" Blackbeard – even though the two never actually met or sailed together.

STICK UP
Captain Blood was based on a book by Italian-born British writer Rafael Sabatini (1875–1950). This poster for the French version illustrates how the film industry transformed the pirate into a romantic hero.

FEARLESS PIRATE FLYNN
In the 1940 movie *The Sea Hawk*, Errol Flynn (1909–59) returned to the role of a swashbuckling pirate hero that had made him famous in *Captain Blood*. As in all his films, Flynn acted even the most dangerous fights, instead of employing a look-alike stunt man, as most other actors did.

Rapier

Index

Acknowledgements

Dorling Kindersley would like to thank:
The staff of the National Maritime Museum, London, in particular David Spence, Christopher Gray, and Peter Robinson; the staff of the Museum of London, in particular Gavin Morgan and Cheryl Thorogood; the staff of the Musée de Saint-Malo; Judith Fox at Wilberforce House, Hull City Museums and Art Galleries; Caroline Townend at the Museum of the Order of St John, London; Elizabeth Sandford at Claydon House, Buckinghamshire; David Pawsey, Mayor Beckwith, Councillor Palmer, and Town Clerk Scammell at Rye Town Hall; Admirals Original Flag Loft Ltd, Chatham; Costume consultant Martine Cooper; French consultant Dan Lallier; Classical consultant Dr Philip de Souza; Brigadier G H Cree for his kind permission to let us reproduce

illustrations from the Journal of Edward Cree; David Pickering, Helena Spiteri, and Phil Wilkinson for editorial help; Sophy D'Angelo, Ivan Finnegan, Andrew Nash, Kati Poynor, Aude Van Ryn, Sharon Spencer, Susan St Louis and Vicky Wharton for design help.
Additional photography by Peter Anderson (12al, ar, cl; 13ar, b), Michele Byam (49cl), John Chase (28cl cr; 31br; 32cl; 33bc; 36bl; 37al, cl, bl; 43ar, c, cr, bl, br; 45al, tr, c, br; 48bl; 62al; 63ar), Stephen Dodd (8br; 9cr; 10cl; 11al, cr, br), Charles Howson (9ar; 22cl; 36ar), Colin Keates (46bl; 52cr), Dave King (61ar), Nick Nicholls (8c; 9b; 10br; 11cl), Richard Platt (34al), Peter Robinson (16cl; 17; 20–21c), James Stephenson (62–63c), Michel Zabé (21ac)
Maps by Eugene Fleury (10cr; 14ar; 20cl; 38cl; 46cl; 54cr)
Endpapers illustrated by Jason Lewis

Picture credits
a=above, b=below, c=centre, l=left, r=right, t=top
Ancient Art and Architecture Collection 7trb; 9tl; 16tl
Bridgeman Art Library, London 18cr; /British Museum 18cl; /Christies, London 53trb; /National Portrait Gallery 18cl; 18cr; /National Maritime Museum 38c
The Master and Fellows of Corpus Christi College, Cambridge 12cb
Delaware Art Museum 49tl
E.T. Archive 21cr; 21br; 22br; 29tl; 39bl
Mary Evans Picture Library front cover br; back cover br; 7tr; 8bl; 12c; 13bra; 15tlb; 18tr; 20tr; 26tr; 35tlb; 35c; 36c; 37tr; 39br; 39tl; 43cb; 47cr; 51tc; 54tr; 54trb; 56cl; 60bl
Kevin Fleming Photography 9tl
Ronald Grant Archive 6tlb; 62bl; 63c; 63tl; 63br; 63cr
Sonia Halliday Photographs 9trb
Library of Congress 26c; 42br
Mansell Collection 40trb; 40bl

Michael Holford front cover tl; 44tl
Cliche Musee de la Marine, Paris 19trb; 51brb
Museum of London 56cra; 57bl
The National Maritime Museum 6tl; 14bl; 14cr; 16c; 22bl; 23tl; 24cl; 25br; 29tl; 29tr; 29cl; 31tr; 32tl; 32bl; 32cl; 33br; 33rc; 33cb; 44bla; 45tc; 45bc; 51tr; 54tr; 54trb; 58trb; 59c; 58br
The National Portrait Gallery, London 60tl
Peter Newark's Historical Pictures15 br; 22cl; 53br
Richard Platt 34tl
Range/Bettman 22tr; 53cr; 52br
Reproduced with the kind permission of The Trustees of the Ulster Museum 29ca
Courtesy of the Trustees of the Victoria and Albert Museum / J Stevenson 63l
Whydah Management Company 41c; 42cl
World's Edge Picture Library 22tl; 49cl
Zentralbibliothek Zurich 13tl